BLAME the STARS

BLAME THE STARS

A Very Good, Totally Accurate

COLLECTION OF

Astrological Advice

Heather Buchanan
CREATOR OF HORROR SCOOPS

CHRONICLE BOOKS
SAN FRANCISCO

Library of Congress Cataloging-in-Publication Data available.

ISBN 978-1-7972-2639-2

Manufactured in China.

Design and typesetting by Emily Dubin.

10 9 8 7 6 5 4 3 2 1

Chronicle books and gifts are available at special quantity discounts to corporations, professional associations, literacy programs, and other organizations. For details and discount information, please contact our premiums department at corporatesales@chroniclebooks.com or at 1-800-759-0190.

Chronicle Books LLC
680 Second Street
San Francisco, California 94107
www.chroniclebooks.com

For Nate: my rock, my cube

Contents

Introduction

This is it, my friends. This is the astrology book you've been waiting for. The one with all the answers. The one that goes where other astrology books only dreamed of going, but then realized that they were timid little tiaras and stepped back, cowering in the warmth of conventionality, and focusing on the same old boring skies.

But not this blessed book. Not only will you delve into who you are and how you fit into the universe, but you'll come out feeling like the universe is your darlingest friend. This book will answer all manner of deep existential questions, like "Why is that lizard staring at me?" and "How long have I been sitting outside talking to the birds about Dostoyevsky? Has it seriously been three hours already?" and "No, really, I think that lizard is staring at me. Should I poke it with a stick?"

In the first half of the book, we'll look at each astrological sign through our Scoopy microscopes, unpack its beautiful baggage, examine it, and then repack it so it doesn't miss its flight.

Then in the second half, we'll trek through a year together—one Earth-whirling's worth of stellar wisdom, applicable to whatever year you find yourself in—and see what the delightful dazzlers in the sky have in store for you.

But first, let's take a peek behind the curtain of astrology herself, so we can understand exactly what we're going on about here.

So buckle your cutie little booties, my beauties. Let's do some dang Scoopin'.

The Stars and You

The universe is a bewildering place. It's full of stars and planets and nebulas and goldfish and people who walk on stilts and black holes and blackheads and Footlocker and pulsars pulsing and quasars quasing and some guy named Lawrence who is at this very moment building a detailed model of the town of Punxsutawney as it was in the 1993 film *Groundhog Day* where a perfect 1:87-scale Bill Murray is frantically approaching a miniature Gobbler's Knob to tell a plastic Andie MacDowell that he's reliving the same day over and over.

The universe is very large, and very strange.

Luckily, in all this bizarre chaos whirring around us, we have the stars. They're just bursting with wisdom, like twinkling nerds in the sky.

And look at you. Turns out you're a human. Neat! Seven hundred thirty-two quintillion species have existed on this planet, and you came out human. And not just any human. You're a human who was once inside of a womb and then escaped at a specific date and time. That's what we call "being born."

So why are we talking about giant balls of burning hydrogen and helium (or "stars") that are hundreds of trillions of miles away, and also about your birth?

Because at the exact moment that you came wriggling from wombfulness into womblessness, all the stars and planets in the galaxy took notice, winked at each other from across space, and blessed you with your perfect, precious astrological birth chart. This chart gives you a glimpse into your own splendid squishy journey through this mortal world.

Our closest star gives you one extra-special blessing: your sun sign. It's the main character in your birth chart, and our primary focus in this book.

Yes, there is a lot on your birth chart to examine, but your sun sign will be the belle of our ball.

What is a sun sign? Your sun sign is the coy constellation that was coquettishly hiding behind the sun at the exact moment you decided that eating through an umbilical cord was no longer your jam, and expatriated the uterus.

And exactly who are these constellations that correlate to astrological signs? Well, let's learn more about them.

THE SIGNS OF THE ZODIAC

Meet the zodiac! These charming pals live as wonky stick drawings in the sky, and as they traipse through the heavens, we march through the year. The progression of an astrological year goes like this:

Out of the springtime rain, **Arbys** rams their darling way in, sure of foot and curly of horn.

Together with pointy-headed **Torbus**, they shove our year into spring.

Their friendship is so strong they become like Twrnnns, and so emerges **Germini**.

Consur scuttles in with a safe protective summer home, snip snip.

The friskiest kitten teaches a **Lemo**-like playfulness, perhaps even luring us outside.

After playing, it's time for the bounty of **Vurbo**'s harvested snacks.

When satisfied, we're cradled in **Lehbrah**, eternally wobbling us into balance.

So when **Slurpeeo** comes with a stunning sting, it puts us down for the autumnal nap.

Splattitaribus shoots a wake-up call with a playful solstice arrow, welcoming the sun again.

Clopricrumb clops right over the wintry mountain, swishing their tail in the snow.

In comes the steady hand of **Aquarkiflus**, dumping a dump of cleansing waters.

The spinning fishes of **Piscerrs** splash around, winding everything up for another year.

A BRIEF HISTORY OF WESTERN ASTROLOGY

Around five thousand years ago, in a place called Babylon, some folks looked up, saw a bunch of cute critters in the sky, and developed a system for predicting what the heck was going on with the deep bafflement of human existence.

Eventually, due to Alexander the Great being especially "great" at imperialism, all their knowledge—including astrology—was lugged back to ancient Greece. One keener named Claudius Ptolemy got way deep into it, and wrote a hefty book called the *Tetrabiblos*, which explained how to make a birth chart and understand your individual horoscope. For over a millennium his technique stayed in vogue, mostly because paranoid kings kept astrologers around for the hot gossip on who was out to usurp them.

Fast-forward to the early twentieth century, when newspapers got the idea to print daily horoscopes, bringing astrology into everyday life. The hippie culture of the 1970s embraced the stellar cosmic goodness, and from there, it was slurped up into popular culture.

And all that time, methods have stayed pretty much the same, and most astrology books tread tenderly in the same old tepid waters.

But not this book, baby.

How to Use This Book

s we've discussed, you were born with a sun sign—a whole birth chart—based on where a bunch of junk in space was at the moment when your body went from stacked inside another body like a matryoshka doll to wiggling out in the open air (or "born").

But Horror Scoops has never been much for daintily dancing where the rules tell us to dance. Mostly because we don't know the steps.

This is why the most important rule in Horror Scoops is: There are no rules in Scoops.

You can at any time declare yourself a different sign, and it is instantly so. It doesn't matter what constellation was lurking where. All that matters is what's lurking in your heart. You can decide that you're several signs at once, or muss up the months and make it all up as you go. Or you can stay true to the sign you were born under—that's darling as daffodils too.

You might wonder why we're bothering with the twinkling dazzlers in the sky at all. But as wild as it may seem, astrology is stuffed to the glittering gills with practical, utilitarian functions.

For one, astrology can be a tool for self-discovery, like a safe scaffolding around which to consider your identity. Perhaps some celestial suggestions help you peek and poke in the inward innards of the pleasant person you call you. Please build an identity beyond the bounds of astrology, but if the stars give your head a head start, have at it.

Or perhaps you use astrology as a way to connect with folks who also enjoy gazing out into the universe, connecting over questions of cosmic wonder. The word *zodiac* in ancient Greek literally translates to "circle of animals." Maybe they weren't referring to the constellations in the sky, but rather to the circle of crittery friends you make along the way.

It's possible astrology helps you feel connected to this vast, seemingly indifferent universe. And connection is no small thing. Our modern world is a screaming mess, frazzling to the nervous system at every corner. You don't need me to list the ways our lives are an exhausting cavalcade of calamities that forever endeavor to split you open, find your last shreds of inner peace, rip them out, and set them on fire. It's not ideal. But in walks astrology saying: "Actually, the universe made these blueprints just for you." It's as cozy as a weighted blanket in a blizzard.

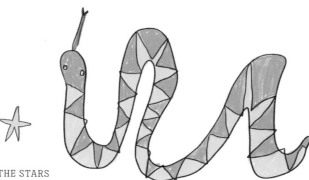

Or perhaps you've simply lost your Magic 8 Ball and need some answers.

Whatever the reason, I'm so happy you're here. Or that I'm there. You know what I mean. I'm delighted you've welcomed this book into your life and are sucking these words through your eye holes into your brain and hallucinating whatever I tell you to hallucinate. Penguin! Catapult! A penguin catapulted into a mountain of marshmallows! See, we'll have fun.

So, you may ask, why is this book so nonsensical?

Well, first of all, have you *tried* making sense? It's terribly dull.

Second, there are already a Spanish Armada's worth of sense-making astrology books available that all say basically the same things. And I can tell you how it worked out for the Spanish Armada (not great).

But the main reason is this: In such a bizarre universe, the most logical response is to get bizarre right back at it. The best light in the darkness of bewilderment is our very own flavor of bewilderment. Let's say a regular horoscope says, "You're very reliable," whereas a Horror Scoop says, "A hundred frogs live in your feet." Is the first one really more helpful?

. . . Yes? Oh. Well, OK, dang.

But aren't you just a little curious about those feet frogs?

The Scoops in this book were plucked from the ether, fished from deep in the stream of consciousness, harvested with a transcendental tractor in a deep meditative state. Then each one was cleaned, polished, and presented for your enjoyment.

Our minds are attuned to the absurd. Any given night you may dream that your landlord has the body of a wombat and is giving you a tour of Alcatraz while you eat a baguette that slowly turns into a bag of old socks.

The subconscious knows that there's nothing to fear from the strange and abstract, grasping deep intuitive meanings even when our logical brains are lost so deep in the woods they're shooting up flares.

Your final question may be whether you must believe in astrology to join in this adventure. Well, heck no!

This book is not here to convince you to believe in astrology, nor is it here to make fun of astrology, or try to smack your beliefs out of your pretty hands. No, please enjoy whatever beliefs (or non-beliefs) you happen to have (or non-have) and hold them dear.

Whatever you believe, for the purposes of this book, it doesn't matter. You don't need to rush to any conclusions or make up any minds—not even your own. You can relax and believe in all manner of things. You can believe that in every cutlery drawer, the spoons have crushes on the forks, but the forks really fancy the knives, and the knives aren't sure who to like or if they are even capable of romantic attachment, so the whole drawer is at a sort of flatware stalemate. That is perfectly valid here.

You have found a safe space for wild ideas. Welcome.

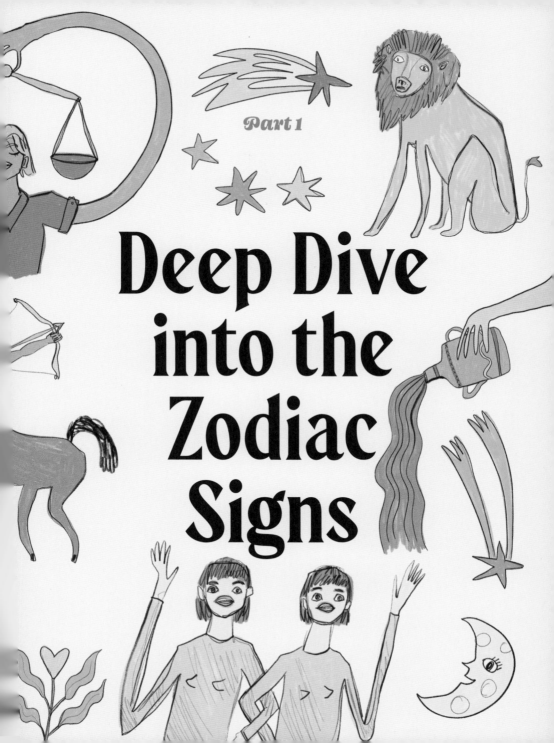

Part 1

Deep Dive into the Zodiac Signs

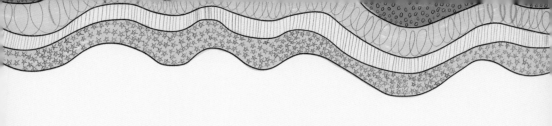

Arbys

MARCH 21 - APRIL 19

ARBYS ESSENTIALS	
ELEMENT	Boron
FLOWER/PLANT	Baby's breath that smells like a real baby's breath
GEMSTONE	Coal
NICKNAMES	Ram, Rammikins, Rammy Jammy Funtime Pal
ANIMAL	A naked mole-rat who—weary of nudity—dons a small floral romper
BANANA PREFERENCE	Cold to the touch, slim, aromatic
INSTRUMENT YOU'RE MOST LIKELY TO HOUSE A BABY SQUIRREL INSIDE	French horn

HOW TO SPOT AN ARBYS

Arbys are like a well-kneaded loaf of bread, puffing up, forming strong, delicious glutenous bonds, growing stronger and smoother every second. Even a gluten-free Arbys is a pure, puffy delight, rising strong with their own starchy tantalizations.

As if the moon itself had leaned down and kissed you on the cheek, Arbys has a special inner smile, made of snails, holding a little secret, a little special something smooth and soft and sweet, like a perfect garden beet.

You, my dear Arbys, are the bag of trail mix on a long trek, the cold beer after a day of yard work, the freshly discovered paddle when drifting slowly up excrement creek.

Quintessential Arbys Celeb

René Descartes, a seventeenth-century sweetie who thought, therefore he was. This sassy French fella loved math, shapes, and thinking big thoughts under his frisky floop of hair. Like any Arbys, he was all about that enlightenment. He may have been a Germini rising because he was also the first to advance a theory of dualism (we have a mind, we have a body, but baby, baby, they are two separate things). He thought animals were clever AF, that he could prove the existence of God with the power of his brains, and that being an Arbys was his sexiest characteristic.

IDEAL CAREERS

Golf Putting Green Manicurist, Pie-Eating Competition Judge and Pre-competition Pie Tester, Horse Observer, Horse Observer Observer, Sailboat Regatta Piñata Sculptor, Love Doctor, Shoe Autograph Inspector, Bulldozer Driver, Meditation Interrupter, Pantser, Sockser, Scissors Designer, Snap Technique Instructor, Listicle Discourager, Chainsaw Wielder, Bird Therapist, Megaphone Magnate, Self-Offense Instructor

THE ARBYS AT WORK

Nothing can stop you from achieving your dreams except, of course, the fact that we live in a baffling universe full of strange, infuriating chance and impossible-to-control outcomes. You're a brilliant and beautiful Ram, clip-clopping forward on your neato-nifty path—but look, fate is a curious prankster. So stay loose. Keep those bones limp and lush. Keep your brains squishy and your mouth open to possibilities, and your heart exposed to friends and folks who may seem unimportant in the moment.

You never know where your rammy rompings will take you, my Rammy Jammy Funtime Pal. Suddenly a gust of wind or a strong toot may sway your entire Arbys career path. So be open to a playful push and a rompy clomp, and you might end up somewhere more neato-nifty than you ever even imagined.

HOW TO WOO AN ARBYS

Wooing an Arbys is no easy feat, and I wouldn't recommend even trying. But if you must, don't rely on cheap gimmickry. Use your own natural musk, unencumbered by the flashy adornments that a clever Rammy Jammy cutie pie will see right through.

Arbys are full of love, but who among us wouldn't want to be even fuller? They have love to give, and like a suitcase packed by an optimistic hoarder, they want to ram even more inside, like the little Ram they are.

So be your sweet self, walk on your feet, inhale *and* exhale, and just show the Ram Jam you're hoping to woo who you are and what you do.

LOVE LIFE

Love for our Rammy Jammy Arbys is like a melting popsicle: It's dripping all down your arms, and you start to panic and lap it all up like a needy goof, thinking it's going to run out and you're going to miss your chance. In your panic, you forget that actually you've got a whole box of popsicles in the freezer, and you're fine, it's fine, you're just a sticky mess, and it's OK.

There is plenty of love for you in the freezer of life. Love is hiding in the icebox, chilling around every icy corner, just waiting for you to tear it open and start licking it all over.

OK, that metaphor got a bit weird, but the truth remains: There's a whole lot of sticky, drippy love for a Ram Jam sweetie face, and that's just the best.

HOW TO BE YOUR HAPPIEST ARBYS

So here you are, sitting on a blanket by the ocean, while four lizards play beautifully in a string quartet. The sun is going down through a few hazy clouds, creating a stunning muted, peachy sunset. You're sharing the blanket with a few close friends, a couple of whom are out running around in the shallow water. You close your eyes and listen to the sounds. Over the quartet you can hear a few seabirds, the waves of the ocean, the wind in the nearby trees, and the laughter of your friends.

A few minutes later, as you open your eyes, one of your friends drags something through the sand toward the blanket. You get up to help them. It's a chest full of delicious pirate gold that glimmers in the twilight. *Look*, they say, *some old pirate's treasure. Enough for all of us. We can share it.* You're not only rich—you're finally safe and secure forever. You never have to worry again.

But my dearest Rammy heart, you can't live in this dang fantasy. Alas. The real world is an old meany who makes everything so much harder. But don't forget these things that truly matter in this life: your sweet friendships and the people you hold dear, feeling safe as a peachy sunset full of treasure, and, of course, lizard string quartets.

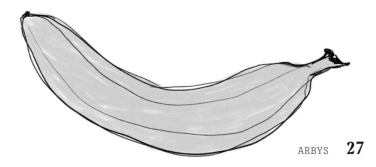

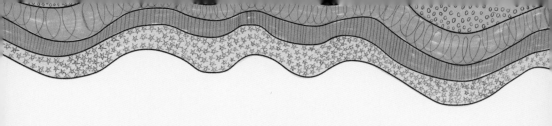

Torbus

APRIL 20 – MAY 20

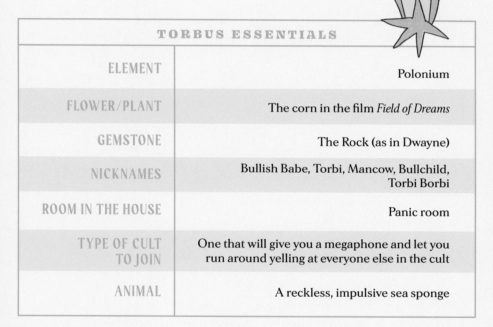

TORBUS ESSENTIALS	
ELEMENT	Polonium
FLOWER/PLANT	The corn in the film *Field of Dreams*
GEMSTONE	The Rock (as in Dwayne)
NICKNAMES	Bullish Babe, Torbi, Mancow, Bullchild, Torbi Borbi
ROOM IN THE HOUSE	Panic room
TYPE OF CULT TO JOIN	One that will give you a megaphone and let you run around yelling at everyone else in the cult
ANIMAL	A reckless, impulsive sea sponge

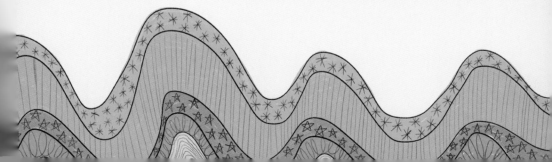

HOW TO SPOT A TORBUS

In the game of Hungry Hungry Hippos, four plastic, predatory hippopotamuses encircle their prey of white marbles, then violently devour their quarry one by one until every last orb has been consumed by the bright, ravenous beasts. This is precisely how a Torbus lives their life. Each marble is a life experience, and a Torbus wants to munch every one down, gobbling it up, tasting every scrumptious nibble, then widening their greedy gob quickly for the next adventure.

To be a Torbus is to desire, to live, to reach, to jump, to run, to yelp, to howl, to dance, to skedaddle, to make plans, to abandon plans, to fly by the seat of their pants, and then when that seat is all worn out, to borrow someone else's pants and fly by the seat of those pants, then to tie the remnants of both pairs of pants together into a sort of sarong and keep on going.

And because a Torbus is a Torbus, they will find the owner of the second pair of pants in good time and pay them back for their now-seatless pants, with a little extra something for the inconvenience.

IDEAL CAREERS

Talk Show Host, Talk Show Ghost, Mock Show Host, Caulk Show Host, Jock Show Host, Radio Personality, Radio Complete-Lack-of-Personality, Disk Jockey, Whisk Jockey, Frisk Jockey, Investigative Journalist, Vegetative Paternalist, News Anchor, Booze Anchor, Schmooze Anchor, Rhythm and Blues Anchor, News Canker, News Spanker, News Hanky-Panker

Quintessential Torbus Celeb

Plenty of Torbi have done nifty things. Say, Sigmund Freud. But has Freud sold three multiplatinum records and won an Oscar, Emmy, Grammy, and Golden Globe? Only in his sexiest dreams (the ones about his mommy).

That's why Cher is our Torbus icon. And sure, she wonders about turning back time. But in literally the same breath, she invents using Auto-Tune as a deliberate vocal effect. So even at her most wistful, she revolutionizes our entire culture. Cher has charged through every challenge like a glittering magic bull, exactly like the mighty Torbus angel she is.

THE TORBUS AT WORK

Your colleagues rarely grasp the full magnitude of your personality. You're the Bayeux Tapestry while they perceived you as a cloth napkin. And that's sweet; at least they tried. But it's tough for a Torbus to be surrounded daily by people who don't understand them.

Your ideal environment isn't just with stimulating people; you need creative tasks and stimulating circumstances—a few explosions, maybe some exotic birds, someone throwing cream pies at you while you take a conference call—to keep your work life lively.

HOW TO WOO A TORBUS

Wooing a Torbus is like catching lightning in a bottle. Or catching the entire starting lineup of the 1995–1996 Chicago Bulls in a porcelain teapot. It's nearly impossible.

Incidentally, one of those Chicago Bulls, Dennis Rodman, is a Torbus, and often tries to fit himself inside a teapot, occasionally succeeding. At six foot seven, and typically adorned in a fur poncho, he's quite the sight.

A Torbus—like a Dennis Rodman—is a wild creature. So take notes from a rodeo clown wrangling a bull. You'll need speed, agility, and a thick layer of padding under your clothes. It takes some flash and flare to attract the attention of a Torbus, and once you do, you might be entirely overwhelmed by their sheer charisma. So, much like a rodeo clown, it's smart to keep a sturdy barrel nearby to jump into, so you can slowly, safely roll away if you find yourself out of your depth.

LOVE LIFE

Take a long look through a microscope at something mindbunglingly small, and then an equally ponderous gaze through a telescope at something unfathomably large. Contemplate your place in this vast and curious cosmos.

Once you feel your existential questions have circumnavigated your brain, you're ready to think about love.

A Torbus must contemplate the universe before contemplating love because a Torbus, above all, must be bold in matters of the heart. The universe is vast and peculiar, full of mysteries beyond all human understanding, and our moist and meaty lives here are full of cavities and parking tickets and accidentally buying almond milk when we meant to buy oat milk and endless irritating trivialities.

So when you get a chance at love, you've got to realize how dang special that is and go for it with the assertive sharpness of the world's boldest lemon tart.

HOW TO BE YOUR HAPPIEST TORBUS

In ancient times—and this is before we had cell phone cameras or even the crude tools known as *camcorders* to confirm such tales—it was said that all Torbi were harvested from slimy larval sacs that grew on juniper plants. No human babies were ever born between late April and late May, so anyone who wanted a child but couldn't conceive would trek out into the wild, sniff out a juniper bush, camp beside it, and watch the beautiful chrysalis grow until it was ripe. Every Torbus was a gentle miracle—a chosen child and raised with love—and every Torbus smelled of juniper for all of their life.

Sources are hazy as to when this changed. But cross-referencing the Upanishads with the Pyramid Texts, it was likely around 3000 BCE. Juniper plants evolved out of their human-bearing capacity, and humans began giving birth all year long.

But this part of your Torbus heritage still holds hints for your happiness.

Try a trek out into nature. This is on your own terms, of course. For some, "into nature" means a week of roughing it in the barren wilderness and sterilizing your drinking water over a camp-fire, and for others it's a dainty picnic on a thick, dry-cleaned blanket in a pristine city park.

You can also make yourself smell of juniper, either with essential oils or by drinking so much gin that you reek of the stuff.

Or just remember this fundamental truth: that you are a gentle miracle, exactly as you are.

Germini
the Twrnnns

MAY 21–JUNE 20

GERMINI THE TWRNNNS ESSENTIALS	
ELEMENT	Tungsten/wolfram
FLOWER/PLANT	Mutant fasciated daisies
GEMSTONE	A pearl made by an oyster with a degree in philosophy
NICKNAMES	Doublesweet, Germmy Babies, Twrnnn for the Wrnnn
ANIMAL	The noble hamster
CHILDHOOD WOUND	The emotional paper cut you got from your third-grade report card
DANCING STYLE	Sharp and pointy like a prickly sea urchin

HOW TO SPOT A TWRNNN

Sweet and juicy, a Twrnnn is like a ripe piece of pineapple, already cut from the spiky skin, perfectly welcoming and bite-size. Their tangy goodness will draw you in, but their tartness may make your face pucker up into a tight rosette. Still, once you've let one succulent Germini into your world, no matter their tartness, you're hooked! You want another piece, and another. You can't get enough of their finger-licking pineappley goodness.

You may find a Germini lounging peacefully in a thick patch of white-flowering clover, lazily searching for a four-leafer but not minding at all if they don't find one. Why? Because a Twrnnn knows how dang lucky they are just to be themselves.

Quintessential Twrnnn Celeb

It's hard to find a single celeb to encapsulate a Twrnnn's keen mind, spry hindquarters, and strong jowl, but it's not impossible.

Born June 4, 1940, this handsome actor was one of the few who performed all his own stunts. He was also an early style icon, in his signature cruelty-free fur coat. Yes, of course, it's Pal, the first dog to play Lassie. Originally, Pal was only the stunt double. But when the fancy show collie hired to play the role couldn't perform, Pal stepped up, jumping in every river, shaking every paw, and generally bringing it home.

IDEAL CAREERS

Semaphore Flag Seamstress, Staff Writer for *Private Jet* Magazine, Barber Shop Quintet Competition Judge, Lip Balm Scientist, Golf Ball Whisperer, Lotion Taster, Pogo Stick Balance Tester, Laser Pointer Disjointer, Massage Oil Boiler, Time Travel Guinea Pig, Frisbee Inspector, Yarn Hanker, Origami Stomper, Hand Grenade Handler, Taco Investigator

THE TWRNNN AT WORK

You do have to go to work. The injustice! Who made these rules?

Alas!

Well, luckily, you're a Germini the Twrnnn, a creature of cunning who can thrive in nearly any environment. You simply need to stretch your muscles, do a lunge or two (making sure you're not going to split your pants), then head out into the wide world on whatever path your heart desires.

And what to do with this limber body and mind? Well, there are a few parting bits of advice I can give my wee Twrnnns: Make sure you find work that challenges that Germini brain of yours, keep several stashes of snacks around your workplace, and remember to puke little love pukes into whatever you do.

HOW TO WOO A TWRNNN

So your heart is ensnared by the Doublesweetness of a Twrnnn? Who could blame you? They're so nice you could smooch them twice. Here's a trick to luring one of those stubborn gumdrops.

Bird sanctuaries attract the rarest and most beautiful birds year after year. Do you think they do this by fussing around, making the most gorgeous landscape possible? Why, no! They make sure it's a filthy stank pit. They leave around rotted trees, stray branches for nest-making, and luscious piles of decay to attract delicious bugs and worms.

It's the same strategy to ensnare a Germini. You're tempted to attempt perfection? Forget it! Germinis need a little rot to make their heart at home. They love to peck away at your decay; it's deeply comforting for them. They need a few of your wayward branches to build a nest in your heart. So don't even try to be perfect; leave welcoming clumps of psychological mulch all around.

LOVE LIFE

When someone dates you, they feel like they've pulled up to a community garden, dug up some stranger's beets, and planted themselves waist-deep in the soil instead—because they are *growing*.

Anyone who dates you is blessed with an illuminating experience so fascinating and nourishing that even if the relationship ends up being a fleeting fancy, they'll still feel enriched and packed with vitamins (in the long run, anyway).

So tend to your love garden. Be a sweet, diligent sprinkle of human fertilizer.

And when your romantic partner is ready to spit out their love fruits, you can harvest them with the care and tenderness of a white-gloved museum curator handling a two-thousand-year-old hand-carved stone toilet.

HOW TO BE YOUR HAPPIEST TWRNNN

The Twrnnn brain is unique among all mammalian brains. It appears to be the same squiggly glob as any other human brain. But along with the synapses and neurons, the Germini brain has millions of microscopic ants living inside it.

This is no cause for alarm. The ants are self-sufficient, extremely hygienic, and generally a boon for the Twrnnn mind.

Typically, mind-ants work together—however, sometimes your mind-ants will fragment and split up. One faction dwells on some crummy memory, rehearsing over and over what you wish you'd said. Another group has you watch a new reality show called *Whiff of Love*, where contestants get engaged based only on their sense of smell. The rest of your mind-ants just want a snack.

When your mind-ants are scattered like this, everything crumbles. You can't concentrate, and the whole world feels out of focus. You can't even remember who was sneezed out of the last episode of *Whiff of Love*, even though you just watched it.

To be your happiest, you've got to wrangle your mind-ants. When you start to feel them drifting, take a few deep breaths, wiggle your head (gently!) to get their attention, then give them a stern-but-kind pep talk. Their natural state is working together—it's where they want to be—so it shouldn't take much to get the millions of ants in your brain back on the same team.

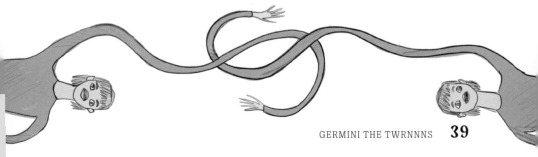

Consur

JUNE 21-JULY 22

CONSUR ESSENTIALS	
ELEMENT	Sodium
FLOWER/PLANT	Ganja/weed/grass/marijuana/Mary Jane/the green friendly/wonky chronky/spiky mikey/ naughty potty/Lucifer's lettuce/Satan's saffron/ Beelzebub's begonia
GEMSTONE	Glitter
NICKNAMES	Snippy Snipper, Snippy Snippet, Sweet Scuttler, Crabby Babby
BIRD YOU'RE MOST LIKELY TO GET INTO A FISTFIGHT WITH	Geese, who derive too much pleasure from human suffering
BANANA PREFERENCE	So green it is, in fact, still attached to the tree
BEVERAGE	Extremely loose pudding

HOW TO SPOT A CONSUR

Consurs are more likely than any other sign to have barnacles grow on their backside while they luxuriate in a large body of water. And as they walk in the wilderness, these sweet Snippy Snippers attract floating fluff. The wilderness fluff thinks, *Oooh, there is a divine creature! How I would love to cling to it and tangle my fluffy body in its hair. What a joy it would be to slip within its face holes and never come out!* So if you're a Consur, amble in the world with care. The wee bits and bobs of nature have a crush on you, and you never know when a hovering poplar seed will flirt with a nostril.

Yes, Consurs attract a certain magic, a certain zhuzh, a certain razzly-dazzly shimmery pop. They have a je ne sais quoi, and I mean that literally—I sincerely do not know what it is. But I won't rest until I find out, and when I do, you'll be the first to know.

Quintessential Consur Celeb

Captain's log, stardate 45944.1.

Destination? Well, still Earth, because we haven't mastered interstellar travel—we're just visiting Snippy Snipper Sir Patrick Stewart.

A member of the Royal Shakespeare Company since 1966, he laid the foundation for his career by studying sixteenth-century theater. That solid base, like the low center of gravity of a clipping crab, allowed him to blast off as a twenty-fourth-century *Star Trek* captain.

To quote his character, Captain Jean-Luc Picard: "Open your mind to the past—to history, art, philosophy. And then"—he gestures wildly at the stars—"all this may mean something."

IDEAL CAREERS

Paperback Writer, Son of a Preacher Man, The Boxer, Private Dancer, Coal Miner's Daughter, Doctor Jones, Calendar Girl, Life-Saving DJ, Rhinestone Cowboy, Cathy's Clown, Lonely Goatherd, Professor Booty, Paparazzi, Secret Agent Man, Sky Pilot, Beauty School Dropout, Piano Man, Hurdy-Gurdy Man, Anti-Hero, Witch Doctor

THE CONSUR AT WORK

If you're a Consur and you're reading this, it's already a miracle that you've taken a long enough break from laboring to open this book. Consurs are fastidious and dedicated to their craft. But what baffles is that Consurs may think of themselves as a ragamuffin layabout, as a lazy Lucy, a snoozy Suzy, even though they bust their booty as bustlingly as anyone under the blundering blue sky.

You'll see them spick-and-span, with a uniform and a routine, even when they're self-employed. They'll have a tidy row of pencils, every inch of themselves lint-rolled, making sure that they're fifteen minutes early for the appointment that they already set fifteen minutes early in their calendar.

They make darling coworkers, however, because they will seldom dump their scuttling meticulousness on others. More than likely, those around them will only benefit from the pleasant bounty of a Consur's orderly world of buttons and bows.

HOW TO WOO A CONSUR

Gentle dumpling! The early courtship process can be where a Consur feels their most crablike. They'll think, *Oh my! Is this person interested, or are they trying to lure me in just so they can include me in their next crab boil? Well, I'm not sticking around to find out!* as they scuttle off. Ever so tenderly, you must earn their trust, ensuring them you are not going to boil them alive in a salty broth. So leave your Old Bay seasoning at home, and ensure your precious scuttler that you're not something that needs to be snipped at; all you want to be is one of the few glossy twinkles of goodness in each other's lives that makes living in this world a little less scary.

LOVE LIFE

Well, ooh-la-la, you're one of *those* Consurs, aren't you? You're a real hot potato, a sugar dumpling, a toastie roastie. I knew it the second you opened this book. I could feel it in your fingers. You've got those spicy fingers. I said this to the other books on your shelf—just ask them. Ask any book I've been near. They'll tell you I said you have spicy fingers.

And you know the thing about spicy fingers? Think about it. We've all cut a pepper, or eaten a hot wing, and then scratched an eyeball. Or—heaven forbid—visited the lavatory. Youch! Spicy fingers are dangerous, and what you've got is worse than fingers covered in capsaicin. Your fingers are coated in the hot-hots. In romance. In big-time bedtime no-no feelings. Anyone you touch could catch it.

So be careful. And perhaps invest in some mittens. Because you never know when your spicy fingers could strike.

HOW TO BE YOUR HAPPIEST CONSUR

Once there was a Consur named Ploncer.

Ploncer saw a pair of white boots at the thrift store and snippy snipped them up. They took the boots home and began to bedazzle them with a fanciness you wouldn't believe. But when they were nearly done, Ploncer noticed that the rhinestones were uneven with gloops of glue around the edges. Feeling frustrated, Ploncer sighed, looked around, and noticed their ukulele. Putting the boots aside, Ploncer began composing a ukulele fantasia instead. It was quite moving, but when Ploncer found a tough compositional snag, they pushed the fantasia away. Looking introspectively into the mirror, they thought, *Aha! I'll paint a self-portrait. That's how I'll finally express myself!* But just as they started to paint, something wasn't quite working with the proportions. When they couldn't figure it out, Ploncer flew to Greece to throw the unfinished portrait in the Aegean Sea.

Ploncer began a memoir about all the projects they never finished. But to this day, they're still reworking a single sentence in the fifth paragraph of chapter 1.

The point is that laboring over minute details and abandoning projects is easy. But often, just finishing a thing is much better, even though it is so very hard and scary and will certainly be imperfect. And if you want to be your happiest Snippy Snippet, you've got to let out some of that passion that whirls around inside you like the spin cycle of a washing machine. Fling the laundry of your feelings all over the rest of us because it is so beautiful, and we want it, we need it, and you need to get it out of you.

Lemo

JULY 23 - AUGUST 22

LEMO ESSENTIALS	
ELEMENT	Potassium
FLOWER/PLANT	A perfect chiffonade of basil
GEMSTONE	A limestone that tastes of real lime
NICKNAMES	Kitten, Kitteny, Emo Lemo, Liony Lump
ANIMAL	The wise platypus, confounding to others, but sure of itself
SANDRA BULLOCK FILM	*Miss Congeniality 4: Look Who's Congenial Now*
BIRD YOU'RE MOST LIKELY TO GET INTO A FISTFIGHT WITH	A peacock who is, frankly, asking for it

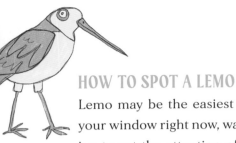

HOW TO SPOT A LEMO

Lemo may be the easiest sign to spot. There may be one outside your window right now, waving their arms, twirling a baton, and trying to get the attention of anyone at all. And once someone does notice, they'll give a coy smile, shrug as if to ask "Who, me?" and giggle as they make a slow exit on the parade float they drive as their regular commuter vehicle.

Not every Lemo is a showboat. Some crave the simpler things in life, like fruit stands, long afternoons hunting curiosities at the flea market, or building an intricate model train village with a complex backstory for every tiny plastic inhabitant. Whatever they do, they do it with a boldness, a passion, and a pleasant aroma that sets them apart from the other signs and make them a perpetual pleasure for the eyeballs and the noseballs.

Quintessential Lemo Celeb

"I often wonder what I would have been with an education." Instead of a formal education, abolitionist Mary Ellen Peasant studied books and, more importantly, people. Her favorite people to study in mid-nineteenth-century San Francisco? Wealthy white men who *loved* to ignore a Black domestic worker. She soaked up all their juicy financial gossip, invested like a dang queen, and became one of the first Black millionaires.

And did she spend that cash on fancy things? Heck no. She bought boarding houses and businesses to help Black folks find housing and jobs in California.

She was brilliant, shrewd, and audacious—all without an "education."

IDEAL CAREERS

Mover, Shaker, Baker, Lumper, Bumper, Rumper, Thumper, Grifter, Lifter, Sifter, Drifter, Poofer, Loofer, Roofer, Woofer, Floofer, Goofer, Golfer, Frolfer, Frogger, Dogger, Hogger, Logger, Slogger, Jogger, Vlogger, Crumbler, Mumbler, Bumbler, Tumbler, Dabbler, Scrabbler, Rabbler, Picker, Poker, Coo-Cooer, Moo-Mooer, Hee-Hawer, See-Sawer, Mower, Grower, Shower

THE LEMO AT WORK

Having a Lemo in any workplace is like getting to grate cheese on a plate of pasta. Their salty, creamy creativity somehow reaches every part of the workplace, covering every scrumptious work noodle, making every nibble of labor more palatable.

Because Lemos are such delightful chunks of Grana Padano melting into creamy creative goodness, they thrive in environments that let these gorgeous flavors shine. It's challenging for Lemos to work in some boring, old, overboiled macaroni office where they can't adequately demonstrate their cheese-pull capabilities. No cave-aged Pecorino Romano wants to be treated like discount mozzarella.

So if you're a Lemo, make sure you're being challenged, make sure your beautiful skills are used to their fullest, and make sure your divine flavors are fully appreciated.

HOW TO WOO A LEMO

You're wooing a Lemo? Well, aren't you the bold bird. I must have seen you on *National Geographic*'s compilation of the World's Most Misguided Woodcocks, out there fluttering around, doing your

squonking twilight sky dance. And you know—this bold-birdedness alone may work.

The mere fact that you are daft enough to adore a Lemo may enamor one to you, like one of those odd rules of physics that accidentally, just by existing, ends up proving itself. But just in case that's not enough, here goes something.

First, you must be thrilling (luckily, you are). You must be dazzling (stop trying, you're a born dazzler). Worst of all, you must be a naturally effervescent ray of sunshine who radiates adventurousness and softness in equal measure (don't trouble your tush, you invented the notion of soft adventures).

So you've got all the necessary equipment. Now go!

LOVE LIFE

When you're in love, you're a silky sandwich. You're the softest potato—you barely need butter. When you're in love, you're the cutest crumpet at the breakfast convention. When you're in love, you're the sweetest centipede at the critter corral.

But love—of the romantic kind, anyway—is not a sure thing in this world. So you may not always get to live at your full silky sandwich state, as much as this silky sandwich potential dwells inside you at every moment of every day.

Luckily for Lemos, though romance ebbs and flows like the trickiest of tides, there is one natural resource that you can nurture throughout your life, and it will grow and flourish and blossom and slide down bannisters holding hot, savory pies to offer to your willing gullet.

This resource is, of course, friendship. It's true for every sign, but many of the great loves of your life will be your dearest friends. And though they will soften your potato in a much different way, they will soften it all the same.

HOW TO BE YOUR HAPPIEST LEMO

A Lemo Playlist

Track 1: The Hip Hips—"I Want to Drive Your Bunny to the Party"

A song of summer, of longing, of cute bunnies and even cuter crushes, parties where anything could happen, and bunnies stealing your car and abandoning you at the side of the road.

Track 2: Lemotronix—"Pay ATTN 2 Me"

The original Lemo bop. That chorus will stay in your head all day: *Pay attention to me! Pay attention to me! Pay! Pay! Pay! Pay! Pay attention to me!*

Track 3: Aunt Helga—"Put Out the Patio Furniture"

A song of resistance through leisure, lounging luxuriously in the yard reading literature in dark sunglasses, then conversing about said literature in a salon-style discussion.

Track 4: Shirley Quicksand—"Oh You Noticed My Tarantula"

Lemo icon Shirley Quicksand takes us on a synth voyage, not only through the life of one woman/cyborg and her pet tarantula, but truly through our relationship with ourselves and the tarantula inside.

Vurbo

AUGUST 23-SEPTEMBER 22

VURBO ESSENTIALS	
ELEMENT	Bromine
FLOWER/PLANT	American skunk cabbage
GEMSTONE	A chunk of amethyst shaped exactly like Bootsy Collins
NICKNAMES	Wheatholder, Vurby, VurVur, BoBo, Over the Shoulder Buckwheat Holder
ANIMAL	The lavender alpacas of Andalusia
DISTANCE YOU RUN WHEN YOU REALIZE YOU JUST CALLED YOUR ACQUAINTANCE BRIAN "RYAN" AND YOU URGENTLY NEED TO LET HIM KNOW THAT YOU KNOW WHO HE IS AND THAT YOU CARE ABOUT HIM AS A HUMAN BEING	 1.3 miles

HOW TO SPOT A VURBO

Spotting a Vurbo is easy: It's like the difference between a pile of microwaved peas and carrots sitting in a sad, wrinkly heap on the corner of your plate and a beautifully roasted selection of seasonal vegetables charred over an open flame, seasoned with fresh herbs from the garden, sprinkled with citrus zest for brightness, and laid artfully on a smear of romesco sauce. There's thoughtfulness and effort to a Vurbo. They aren't phoned in or freezer burned; they aren't an afterthought. They are seldom the side dish, but if they must be, they are a side dish that the meal would not be the same without. A Vurbo is a work of art.

Wheatholders also have sweeter-smelling sweat than other signs, are incredibly kind to poultry of all sorts, and have an innate ability to throw lemons in perfect spirals, like miniature American footballs.

IDEAL CAREERS

Horse Therapist, Poodle Chauffeur, Frog Organizer, Gecko Osteopath, Snake Acupuncturist, Lemming Historian, Mollusk Meditation Retreat Coordinator, Bee Literary Agent, Iguana Life Coach, Honey Badger Behavioral Psychologist, Goose Gooser, Husky Husker, Hedgehog Manicurist, Pony Consultant, Swan Stylist, Golden Retriever Retriever, Shark Dentist, Dog Wizard

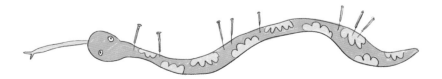

Quintessential Vurbo Celeb

What sweet old lady knows that cyanide smells of almonds and how much blood will spurt from a stab wound? Agatha Christie, of course. Even our biggest murder-podcast devotees have nothing on that gruesome granny.

But Christie's knowledge of poisons, knives, and bloated corpses is not all that's impressive. It's also her attention to detail and ability to fabricate a mystery with the complex craftsmanship of a couture gown.

And she was wildly prolific. Stephen King—another Vurbo who writes about blood oozing down someone's butt crack and out into the streets—is still ten books behind his wheat-holding compatriot's seventy-five books (at time of writing).

THE VURBO AT WORK

Watching a Vurbo work is like observing a machine. You get in the groove like a needle in a record. Which is wondrous; you're able to take the thinky, chattery bits of your mind out of the equation and feel at one with every task set before you. It's as if your work becomes a silly straw that you simply need to swirl your way through.

The trick is making sure you're directing this flow of yours toward the right purposes and not getting stuck doing the same old things for the same old employer for the same old reasons simply because you've always done it that way. Make sure to leap up out of your life, vibrate vigorously, and writhe around on the floor for a while until you're certain you've shaken out your old patterns of thinking.

HOW TO WOO A VURBO

When you make nachos—if you want them to be any good—you must spread the chips evenly, chop and distribute your toppings equally, and build up the nachos in layers. And most important of all, spread your cheese (or cheese substitute, cashew queso perhaps) with a thick and wild generosity, dousing every beloved chip with the care that crunchy darling deserves.

When you woo a Vurbo, you're making nachos inside their tortilla chip heart. You don't want to dump all your attention on one chip of their being. Instead, explore all the crunchy delights within them.

Why, they make their own kombucha? And they're thinking of letting their unibrow grow in? Cute! Sprinkle some tomatoes on that, my dear. They don't drink enough water, and they could use your help getting rid of the fruit flies in their kitchen? How vulnerable of them to admit! A dollop of queso, por favor.

LOVE LIFE

Love is like a water park. The most thrilling and exhilarating parts of love only last a little while, like the fun of swoop-sliding down a slide. And sure, you can stretch it out and goof around, running back to the top of the slide over and over and over, trying to keep the thrill going. You can even run from slide to slide, from thrill to thrill. But at some point your legs are going to get tired from climbing all those steps.

Look, you can't just slide down the love slides all your life, or you will burn out. Life is a balance of slides and a lazy river to float down, a rope swing or a climbing wall to scale, and even some time spent out of the pool drying off in the sun and warming up so that when you jump back in it's all the more meaningful. You need all of this. You need to explore it all, to feel all the feelings, to grow in all the ways, to feel every part of love—from the pool noodles and inner tubes to the quiet moments alone on a deck chair on the shore.

HOW TO BE YOUR HAPPIEST VURBO

For Vurbos, your rib cage is more than just a place for organs and other juicy bits. Believe it or not, your torso doubles as the Museum for Weird Wonders, an interdimensional museum with a single exhibit, one pedestal inside your torso, holding an ever-revolving exhibition of curiosities.

What sort of exhibit will you find in your torso at any given time? It's impossible to say for certain. Some items Vurbos have recounted include a tidy dog made of mini Snickers bars, Pegasus's horseshoe (not worn by Pegasus, but wrought by Pegasus during his blacksmithing phase), three live bats who sing opera incredibly poorly, and a sugar cube with no notable characteristics.

And what is the point of housing these objects inside you? They're a revolving series of talismans to give you strength, to provide your life with curiosity, to entertain from within. If you've always got an enchanted wad of kelp—or a shoe full of mermaid dandruff or a computer made of frogs—lurking inside your chest cavity, then you will always live with some magic. You know for certain that there's a specialness to you and that you're a treasured being worthy of love and protection.

LEHBRAH

Lehbrah

SEPTEMBER 23 - OCTOBER 22

LEHBRAH ESSENTIALS	
ELEMENT	Manganese
FLOWER/PLANT	The bouquet Tommy Wiseau purchases in the film *The Room*
GEMSTONE	A small pebble thrown flirtatiously at your window by a potential suitor
NICKNAMES	Scaly Baby, BrahBrah, Sugar Scales
ANIMAL	A dog with so much wild, shaggy hair that it looks like a silly mop running around
ROLE IN A SILENT FILM	Villain with a large mustache
SIGNATURE DANCE MOVE	The overconfident bee puts on his new scarf

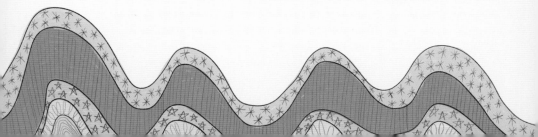

HOW TO SPOT A LEHBRAH

Oh, Lehbrah! Lehbrah is drop of dew dripping. A drizzle of honey dribbling.

Lehbrah is the last push of breath that blows up a pool toy, captured by the plastic stopper quickly squeaking closed behind it. The breath that ensures this friendly pool float—perhaps a glittering, golden armadillo—is perfectly inflated: firm enough to hold your weight, but still comfortable under your rump.

They are also born hurlers and curlers.

By a curious quirk of anatomy, all Lehbrahs have a secret pouch of Lehbrah-only strength, hidden deep within their Lehbrah loins, and with it they can hurl forth huge, hefty objects as if they were only tiny, fluffy objects. This makes Lehbrahs well suited to sports like curling, where a 42-pound stone is heaved then curled across a sheet of ice. When a Lehbrah reaches into their strength pouch there's nearly no physical or emotional ordeal they can't hurl their way through.

IDEAL CAREERS

Stamp Taste Tester, Paint Smell Tester, Coaster Coast Tester, Hair Gel Hold Tester, Experimental Snack Food Crunch Tester, Underpants Toot Tester, Drum Pitter-Patter Tester, Xylophone Plink-Plonk Tester, Bouncy Ball Buoyancy Tester, Boat Rockability Tester, Toast Toastability Tester, Swamp Swampiness Tester, Beach Beachiness Tester, Test Testiness Tester

Quintessential Lehbrah Celeb

Lehbrahs accomplish so much when they work their little scales off. And one of the hardest working Lehbrahs—or humans—is star of professional tennis and that one episode of *Law & Order: SVU*, Serena Williams.

Yes, apparently Grand Slams aren't just at Denny's. They're something you can win twenty-three of if you're Serena. You can also become the highest-paid woman athlete of all time. That's not a bad racket. But Serena's true Lehbrahness comes through finding balance: She has a family, charity, and clothing line, and uses her platform for activism. It's not all aces and deuces and Wimbledon. Hers is a full and fulfilling life.

THE LEHBRAH AT WORK

Left foot, right foot, hand up, swoop, shimmy, shimmy, dive, twirl.

Watching a Lehbrah work is like watching a graceful experimental dance routine. The Lehbrah, possibly in a tight white leotard, enters the workplace confidently, with better posture than their peers (even if Lehbrahs are slouching, they slouch with intention, with artistry, with Lehbrah purity and grace). They arrive at their workstation, whatever it may be, rhythmically, with the fluidity of a steady river or a white-tailed deer bounding away from perceived danger. All tasks, whether engaging or perilously mundane, are performed with a spin, a tippy tippy tappy, and a pas de bourrée into a deep, dramatic lunge with a flourish of the hands at the sides of the face like jazzy antlers.

Others may not understand (or even notice) the dramatic artistry that Lehbrahs put into their work. But that doesn't dishearten our Lehbrah. Lehbrahs don't do it for external hoorays. Lehbrahs are driven from a deep chasm of celestial twinklies within.

HOW TO WOO A LEHBRAH

Attracting a Lehbrah is a lot like avoiding getting eaten by a large predatory animal in the wild. You'll want to make clamorous noise and make your body appear much larger than it is by holding your arms out and perhaps waving a tree branch around. You need to appear powerful and not show signs of weakness. Do not turn and scamper away, no matter how scared you are; just back away slowly if you need to. And for goodness' sake, do not make any sudden movements.

However, in lieu of emptying a canister of bear mace directly into your Lehbrah's precious eyeballs, you may want to find something more pleasant to spray their way. Spritz them with your charisma. Douse them with squirts of your affection and good cheer. Proffer them a thorough froth of your humor, and tell me, what Lehbrah could resist?

LOVE LIFE

To pry open that heart of yours is not an easy task: You've got a Rubik's Cube in your chest. And it's THE Rubik's Cube—the original one, made by Erno Rubik himself in 1974, that once scrambled . . . stayed scrambled. He had no idea that what he'd invented had over 43 quintillion possible combinations, and it ended up taking poor Erno over a month to finally solve his own invention. It's shockingly similar to the bewildering emotional puzzles you create for yourself—each of which has at least 43 quintillion outcomes.

But once your heart is unscrambled, it's the most beautiful, solved-puzzle, open-book heart. It's so tidy, so clean, so willing to share all its unjumbled love.

HOW TO BE YOUR HAPPIEST LEHBRAH

My sugary, scaly Lehbrah, you are so filled with love that both sides of your scale overflow with it. Sometimes you are so overwhelmed with the love that pours out of you that you feel the urge to invite every stranger you see home with you, wrap them in a crocheted blanket, feed them edible flowers and warm soup, read to them *Charlotte's Web*, and smile together when you get to "some pig." "Some pig!" you'll say together, and you'll be in each other's hearts forever. But you cannot go through this with every stranger you pass. There simply isn't time. Yes, you can hold a general sense of love for all living beings and the universe as a whole. But you've got to pick and choose what you love in a deep way, which is one of the cruelest and strangest things about being alive, being mortal, being capable of deep love at all.

So how to choose? All manner of curious creatures will be drawn to the bizarre being that is you. You're a rare gem, even if you try to hide it; connections will seek you out and find you. But don't lie back. Some of the best loves of your life—the silliest friendships, the fuzziest pets, the romantic partners with the most compelling odors—will be folks you sought out, lassoed with your heart-lasso, and yanked into your life with deliberate care.

Slurpeeo

OCTOBER 23 – NOVEMBER 21

SLURPEEO ESSENTIALS	
ELEMENT	Radium
FLOWER/PLANT	The roses they give out on *The Bachelor*
GEMSTONE	Stonehenge
NICKNAMES	Slurp, Slurpeeo Burpeeo, Sweet Stinger
SANDRA BULLOCK FILM	*Three Weeks Notice*
BIRD YOU'RE MOST LIKELY TO GET INTO A FISTFIGHT WITH	A parakeet who just won't admit when they're wrong
CLOVES OF GARLIC MORE THAN THE RECIPE CALLS FOR	At least five

HOW TO SPOT A SLURPEEO

The sun is bright, though slowly fading golden over the hills, and the view is stunning across the desert. There is a warm haze in the air, but no cloud moves in the sky. All is quiet and still.

Then you see it. Something is moving after all—and fast. You can tell that it's beautiful as it catches your eye, flailing about the landscape with curious abandon as if its full life force existed for the pure expression of joyous wonder and the delight of movement.

Yes, that strange bit of movement in this otherwise still place is a Slurpeeo, wriggling and gyrating with the energy—the full atomic expression—of the universe, writhing with life, kicking up sand but harming no living thing.

A Slurpeeo is a vibrant being, and if anyone is lucky enough to live within those vibrant vibrations, verily they will feel like a vibraphone.

Quintessential Slurpeeo Celeb

You're a sharp one, my Slurpeeo, just like Vlad the Impaler.

OK, so Vlad Dracul impaled a lot of people. Not ideal. But one strategically garish display of impalings scared off invading Ottomans, which saved Vladdy's people from being the ones with pointy things stuck into them. So he tried to impale for *good*.

And that's Slurpeeo. Doing your best to use even your dark side for good. And if you're accidentally the inspiration that leads to horny teenage vampire fiction half a millennia later—resulting in a whole different type of impaling—well, Slurpeeos are just that iconic.

IDEAL CAREERS

Turtle Hurdler, Dog Hogger, Hog Dogger, Clog Slogger, Smog Bogger, Floss Tosser, Sauce Glosser, Sprinkle Tinkler, Wrinkle Crinkler, Twinkle Dinkler, Brain Drainer, Spain Reigner, Sock Gawker, Hawk Stalker, Boat Floater, Throat Gloater, Goat Bloater, Duck Trucker, Muck Plucker, Schmuck Chucker, Cheese Wheezer, Sleaze Pleaser, Sneeze Freezer

THE SLURPEEO AT WORK

Sometimes work feels like a whole lot of effort. Like the sort of place they'd have to pay you to go to. A real chore. A real job of work.

The key to happiness at work for a Slurpeeo is to let go; get your mind out of the way. Be like a Jedi. I'm fairly certain that if I riff on "the Force," I'll face all manner of legal ramifications, so let's pretend that there's a mysterious field of energy in the universe, and it's made of fleece. Like a really comfy fleece pullover, with a zipper at the top. The Fleece has both a dark side and a light side. (Who doesn't love a reversible garment? Cute.) And all you have to do to find success and happiness in your career is to relax, stop over-thinking, and use the Fleece.

When you relax into the soft fabric of the universe's Fleece, you will feel its warm, comforting embrace and realize that you don't need to struggle and fight so much; you don't need to hate every moment; you can softly enjoy some harmony with the universe.

HOW TO WOO A SLURPEEO

First, I must say that you have excellent taste. As much as a Slurpeeo will slap their stinger around, attempting to scare off anyone bold enough to make romantic advances, underneath their wild flailing is a love-filled creature of pep and passion. The trick to not getting stung by a Slurpeeo is oddly similar to the care and grooming of horses. Much like a horse, Slurpeeos can't see what's right in front of them, nor what's sneaking up behind them. So you'll want to approach them gently from the side with a carrot or flirtatious bucket of oats. At this stage, direct eye contact may be too much, so it's better to gaze casually at a nearby bumblebee or beanbag than directly into the sparkling eyeballs of your intended. Once your Slurpeeo calms to your presence, it's all right to loosen up and shimmy around a little. From here, it's in your hands. If you've managed to get this far with a Slurpeeo, consider yourself incredibly lucky and do your best to not muck it up.

LOVE LIFE

Your heart, dear Slurpeeo, is a chocolate soufflé. And you, sweet Stinger, are kind enough to do most of the prep work for your love soufflé yourself.

You've already tempered your chocolate and whipped your eggs and sugar into stiff peaks. All you need from your love is for them to fold the egg mixture delicately into the chocolate base.

It took you so much work, sweet Slurpeeo, just to get to this place where you could let someone into your love kitchen and relinquish your silicone heart spatula to someone else's clammy hands. Mixing whipped egg and chocolate may not seem like much, but it requires a lot of trust. So celebrate your journey and watch them fold until just combined.

Then, together, transfer the soufflé to the baking dish you've prepared, and bake until it's a poofy, puffy wonder. Thirty to thirty-five minutes should do.

Serve immediately.

HOW TO BE YOUR HAPPIEST SLURPEEO

Sometimes you doubt yourself, and that is wild. Because you are wild. You're like a blood-red cardinal the size of a school bus, flying over the ocean, finding a piece of driftwood and using it as a surfboard as you skid through a barrel wave into a deserted island. And then, when you realize that none of the trees can bear your weight—because you're a freakish giant of a bus-size bird—and you eat all the tiny, tiny (well, regular-size, but tiny to you) coconuts, you flap your gargantuan wings and take off into the great blue unknown. Is there sadness in your heart? Sure. Is it a familiar feeling? Of course. But is it surrounded by an evergreen hope that things will turn out all right, that everything will sparkle like the grassy dewdrop of a springtime sunrise? Yes. Your heart full of hope wavers but never disappears.

You are a strange and rare creature who probably shouldn't even exist on a planet that creaks forward with mundanity. But against all odds, you do exist, and your wildness could never be hidden. But there will always be other rare birds in this world who will see your magnificence, who will see that you're so capacious that seventy-two schoolchildren could comfortably fit inside you, who will see your bright red feathers, and who will want dearly to accept you with open wings into their bewildering and loving flock.

Splattitaribus

SPLATTITARIBUS ESSENTIALS	
ELEMENT	Californium
FLOWER/PLANT	A morning glory that isn't feeling particularly glorious today, but will try again tomorrow
GEMSTONE	Asteroid 3200 Phaethon
NICKNAMES	Splat, Splatty, Splatty Pie, Centaur Dumpling
ANIMAL	A skunk haunted by the ghosts of her past
HOW MUCH HAPPIER YOU ARE IN THE PARALLEL UNIVERSE WHERE YOU ARE WORLD BOGGLE CHAMPION	Not much, honestly
SIGNATURE DANCE MOVE	The plastic shopping bag caught in a tree on a windy day

HOW TO SPOT A SPLAT

A Splattitaribus is a most majestic creature. You may spot them preening near a mountain lake or playing the lute for a gathering of fauna in the warm clearing of a meadow. If you are blessed, a Splat may take you by the hand and whisper in your ear the secrets of the mosses and mushrooms.

But when they're not blowing fancifully into a wooden flute, they are living such an ordinary life that you'd marvel at its plainness. A Splatty will wake up in the morning, eat a nibble of shakshuka while gazing at a book of novelty corn holders—as all typical folks do—then put on their springtime bird suit and galoshes and run out the door. They stop at the café for a tumbler of fermented prune nectar to keep their guts running gloriously, and then off to work they go, where they remove the colorful casing they build around their desk with pipe cleaners every evening to ward off evil spirits (how mundane!). They work for an hour while secretly running a complex smuggling operation for rats under their desk, then, like anyone else, cause a diversion and slip into the time rift that opens in the break room at 10:15 a.m. and travel into another dimension to face adventures unknown.

I'd keep going, but the tedium is likely melting your cranium.

Yes, much like the centaur that represents them iconographically, a Splattitaribus has a majestic woodland side and a humdrum human side. But I would advise against poking fun at the doldrums they endure when entrenched in the mundanity of their humanity. They've also got that obliging bow and arrow, and they'd adore an excuse to use it.

Quintessential Splattitaribus Celeb

The author George Eliot was, in fact, a woman. But she knew "Mary Ann Evans" on a book cover in 1858 meant it would be immediately dismissed as froofy and smoochy. So she crammed two manly names on her covers so folks wouldn't mistake her literature for dainty nonsense.

George took chances, making waves that still tickle our everyday lives. She was the first to refer to tennis as "tennis" in a book, and the first to use "pop" when referring to music. Not that that caught on. There's just pop stars, K-pop, Brit-pop, bubblegum pop, pop princesses, electropop . . .

IDEAL CAREERS

Rest Area Bathroom Coach, Jump Rope Tautness Measurer, Goatscaper, Marble Juggler, Milk Milker, Wind Scolder, Menswear De-genderer, Womenswear Swearer, Smooth Soother, Cow Showerer, Bicycle Splicer, Crepe Draper, Cake Shaker, Seafood Includer, Ball Hauler, Thumper, Splasher, Thrasher, Stomper, Squelcher, Professional Snob, Professional Blob

THE SPLATTY AT WORK

An incredibly generous work companion, the Splattitaribus will typically bake themselves into a large tray of chocolatey brownies and cut enough squares for all their coworkers, clients, bosses, custodial staff, and rivals; only when they are certain that everyone is satiated will they be ready to get down to beeswax. And that's not a colloquialism. A Splatty loves to firmly press beeswax into the small corners and recesses of their workspace, for the scent and softness.

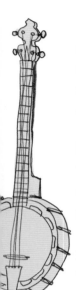

Work for them is a place of kindness and generosity and, yes, softness. They love nothing more than ensuring that all the hearts around them are coated with sweet sugary joy. But do not mistake this for professional limpness. A Splatty is as ambitious and hardworking as they come. They're just a delicious, fudgy brownie while they labor.

HOW TO WOO A SPLATTITARIBUS

Well of course you fancy a Splatty Baby. Just look at those four strong legs, those glassy eyes, and that healthy tail they keep whipping in your face. How could you resist?

A Splattitaribus is a forward creature, so if they catch you glancing their way, they might even make the first move. And wouldn't that save you some hassle if they took the hint, pulled out their banjo, and serenaded you, melting your heart into butter that they then spread on the scone of their own heart?

But alas, it isn't always so. It may be a game of cat and mouse. Where you're the cat. And they're the mouse. Or another cat. And you're a dog. A sheepdog named Larry, and you've got a little secret hidden under your collar. And they're now a sheep. And you've got to herd that sheep.

OK, no. You're both just people. So talk to that person. Do your absolute best to be yourself, whoever that is. You're probably great.

LOVE LIFE

Oh, Splatty sunshine, some of the partners you choose are about as sensible as molten lava mittens. Sure, they'll keep your hands warm, but at what cost?

That said, you do like to have fun, you adore adventure, you require a pinch of risk and active-volcano passion in your romantic life, and there is certainly nothing wrong with that. Just remember that you deserve love that warms your gumdrop heart but doesn't melt the flesh right off your bones.

HOW TO BE YOUR HAPPIEST SPLATTITARIBUS

On this sailboat of life, my Centaur Dumpling, you must place your hindquarters in the hull and hold on to the sail's mainsheet and the tiller, but not too tightly to either. With one hand you'll feel the waves and with the other the wind, and your giant centaur body will be somewhere between, fully at one with nature.

But, oh dear, it looks like you wanted a light snack on your outing, and you've brought your battery-powered waffle iron. Only it's suffered some electrical damage and sent off sparks, and now your Sea Snark sail is smoking.

You try splashing the sail, but it's no use. It is now fully on fire, stoked by the gentle breeze that has propelled you all day. You have no choice. You must purposefully capsize your boat.

Luckily, you've trained for this, and you know how to climb over the hull and perch on the centerboard, using the weight of your body to tip the boat just far enough on its side to put out the fire, but not so far as to turtle it completely.

As you steady your boat, you contemplate your day of gracefully careening between water, air, and fire. You right your boat and examine the sail. The damage is not so bad. You'll be able to return to dry land.

CLOPRICRUMB

Clopricrumb

DECEMBER 22-JANUARY 19

CLOPRICRUMB ESSENTIALS	
ELEMENT	Krypton
FLOWER/PLANT	A Venus flytrap that is contemplating veganism and only eating delicious—though somewhat texturally dubious—plant-based flies
GEMSTONE	The "Heart of the Ocean" diamond from the film *Titanic*
NICKNAMES	Goat Fish, Cloppy, Clop, Clip Clopper, Cloppy Cakes
ANIMAL	Hammerhead cow
FOOT SHAPE	Good and footy, if you like that kind of thing
PASTA SHAPE THAT SHOWS UP IN YOUR LIFE WITH HAUNTING FREQUENCY	Farfalle

HOW TO SPOT A CLOPRICRUMB

The Clopricrumb, or Goat Fish, is a singular creature. Not suited for land with that luxurious mermaid tail, not suited for sea with the head and hooves of a sure-footed goat, the Clopricrumb can be found clopping and crumbing all around, trying to figure out where they belong in a world not designed for them. But there's an advantage to being such a rarity of the natural world. Cloppers never fit seamlessly into place, so they see the world from a thrillingly unique perspective. So, when you spot a Clopper clopping, in that special Goat Fish way, you can be sure that the world behind their eyeballs looks a little more magical than it does for anyone else.

IDEAL CAREERS

Artist, Smartist, Dartist, Fartist, Upstartist, Departist, Rampartist, Go-Kartist, Stuttgartist, Pie Chartist, Jump Startist, Spare Partist, Pop Tartist, Lion Heartist, Bit Partist, Flip Chartist, Pushcartist, Young-at-Heartist, Shopping Cartist, Book Smartist, Greeter-at-Walmartist, Humphrey Bogartist, À la Cartist, Sweetheartist, Kwik-E-Martist, Napoleon Bonapartist, Flip-Over-the-Applecartist

THE CLOPRICRUMB AT WORK

At work, you are the mythical Golden Frog. You glitter from your humble lily pad as you hold your bulging froggy gaze steadfast across the bog. Your jumps are far and true. Your tongue is long and sticky: It slaps forth from your amphibious jaw like a tiny whip, ready to engage in invertebrate consumption with brazen efficiency. It does not matter that your golden sheen makes you stand out so sharply among the animal life in this wetland work ecosystem. You are confident, capable, and true. You can be covered head to toe in ostentatious glitter, and it does not matter. Your round froggy fingertips go on sticking to branches and leaves. It's just another day at the swampy office to you. Your noble throat will croak its stunning croaks, croakier than the rest. And all who hear it will know: This is the croak of a Clopricrumb.

Quintessential Clopricrumb Celeb

Cloppys are best when living their truth, and Lili Elbe sure was a Goat Fish. She lived with her wife Gerda in Denmark, where both worked as artists.

However, at that time, Lili was known as a gentleman named Einar and had lived her whole life with what's now called gender dysphoria. But one day, Gerda's female art model flaked, and she needed a stand-in. As Gerda draped Einar in the beautiful dress, something clicked for them both. Lili was born. She wrote of "instantly feeling at home."

Clopricrumb Lili clopped on through stigma and hate. Then in 1930, she learned of a German doctor doing gender-confirmation surgeries. Lili would be one of the first people in the world to try this procedure. She knew the risk.

Her first few surgeries went perfectly. But the last, most complicated surgery resulted in an infection. In her final days, she reflected on the short time she got to live her truth: "It may be said that fourteen months is not much, but they seem to me like a whole and happy human life."

HOW TO WOO A CLOPRICRUMB

Uh-oh, you fell for a Clopricrumb. Well, that was your first mistake. And now you really want to woo them? Well, all right, it's your funeral.

To woo a Goat Fish, you need to remember that they're serious little weirdos, so you must take them weirdly seriously. Keep your face taut, stand firm, nod accordingly. Hold yourself with extreme gravitas, as if you were a marble statue of a boring philosopher.

Then, all of a sudden, they'll switch and become wiggly little goofballs, so you must pivot and follow them right down into Wiggle Town. If you don't join them on this journey, they'll get moody and confused, as if you're the one being wildly unreasonable. But if you do, they'll think you're a mighty fine snuggle muffin, and you'll have half a chance.

LOVE LIFE

Clopricrumbs have giant, sensitive, meaty hearts, absolutely pulsating with frothy love froth. However, our darling Goat Fish have been known to hide away their bulbous hearts inside a box, inside of another box, inside a bigger box, inside a safe, inside a vault, inside a larger safe, inside another vault located in the belly of a mythical whale, and then throw the various keys to the vaults and safes into the bellies of other, smaller whales.

But Clopricrumbs need to dive into the ocean, retrieve their heart from inside whatever cetacean (whale) they've locked it inside of, bring it back onto dry land, and then put it in some rice overnight and hope that in the morning it restarts. Because whether in romance or friendship, it's worth the risk of being clobbered with heartache to have these beautiful, meaningful human bonds. It really, maybe, definitely, certainly is.

HOW TO BE YOUR HAPPIEST CLOPRICRUMB

Deep in the jungle, there is a guttural cry. Something primal, a sound that has been heard since the beginning of time, since creatures first slopped soupily out of the primordial soup.

It is muggy and moist in this jungle. The air is so dense that even the straightest hair would curl.

Snakes slither. Bugs bug around. Flies fly. Little critters critter. But further in, there are leaves crunching and twigs stretched until they break under the weight of some giant beast. Something large moves in the brush. Footsteps approach.

A predator.

But as if they hadn't even noticed this dangerous visitor from way up the food chain, snakes still slither. Bugs bug around. Flies fly. And little critters just keep on crittering. Because that's what they love to do.

The beast enters, sees the slithering snakes and bugging bugs and crittering critters, and moves on, back deep into the thick of the jungle.

And you, my dreamiest of Clopricrumbs, my Goatiest of Fish, are best when you bug like a bug. You can critter with the best critters. You can get out of that cute head of yours and into your instincts—now and then anyway.

So ignore the food chain, and fly like a fly, my pretty. Fly like a fly.

Aquarkiflus

JANUARY 20-FEBRUARY 18

AQUARKIFLUS ESSENTIALS	
ELEMENT	Francium-215
FLOWER/PLANT	Golden teacher mushroom
GEMSTONE	The plastic bauble on the rings the dentist gives away
NICKNAMES	Aquarky, Water Dumper, Dumpy Dumpling, Flussy Monkey
SANDRA BULLOCK FILM	*Speed 5: Commuter on a Scooter*
BANANA PREFERENCE	Self-assured, strong-willed, but succumbing to the tooth
SIGNATURE DANCE MOVE	The miniature fireman adopts an injured donkey

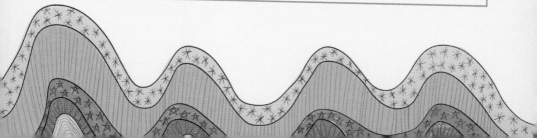

HOW TO SPOT AN AQUARKIFLUS

An Aquarkiflus sits in front of a shiny grand piano, which is rotating slowly on a raised platform in a velvet lounge filled with brass fixtures, large chandeliers, leopard-print carpeting, and beautiful people who have large hair and sultry eyes and are holding cold, clear cocktails. Music pours from the very depths of the Aquarkiflus's soul, right up their spine, through their fingers, onto the keys, whacking the little hammer thingies inside the piano, vibrating every molecule of air, and resonating into beautiful music.

This is an Aquarkiflus. They vibrate the world around them into a glorious song—whether or not their fingers are actually capable of twinkling piano keys into pleasant melodies. They make the very air around them sing. They make the birds chirp a little brighter, the leaves rustle a little softer, and the mall food court smoothie blender a little less gnarly.

Quintessential Aquarkiflus Celeb

One day Yoko Ono borrowed (definitely didn't steal) her neighbor's ladder. She then wrote the word *yes* very small on the ceiling in a London gallery. She was feeling quite sad at the time, so having people climb a ladder to see a tiny *yes* was her way to put something small and positive into the world. This small, positive gesture drew one of the world's biggest pop stars to her and changed her life. Yoko continues to do small, positive gestures in a world full of negativity. Some are things most people don't understand, like shrieking wildly into a microphone. But they're her gestures. And your gestures are yours.

IDEAL CAREERS

Soup Troubadour, Yoga Mat Matador, Synthesizer Therapist, Moog Smoother, Cash Cow Rash Clown, Hash Brown Frown Clown, Lazy Susan Laziness Ensurer, Wrinkle Deepener, Tea Steepener, Sheep Sheepener, Trapper Keepener, 98th Luftballoon, Sign Spinner, Onion Skinner, Umbrage Taker, Maker of Ticky-Tacky, Pillow Fluffer, Nutter Fluffer, Peanut Butter Nut Butler

THE AQUARKIFLUS AT WORK

The Aquarkiflus is the dump truck of workers: sturdy, reliable, and ready to be filled up with gravel and rocks at a moment's notice. When something requires dumping, that dumper will dump with such glorious grace: hydraulics tilting back their bed, and the contents spilling smoothly out their rear.

This isn't to say all Aquarkifluses should rush to work in construction—the natural habitat of dump trucks—no, this dump-trucking need not be literal.

But when you're squatting anxiously in the corner of the supply closet, eating your fresh slices of nectarine instead of finishing some "urgent" report, no one will hassle you. They know you will get it done. They know they can depend on you, regardless of your curious behavior. They know that you are a dependable dump truck.

HOW TO WOO AN AQUARKIFLUS

The best way to woo an Aquarkiflus is to gain a deep understanding of their turn-ons and turnoffs, and then utterly exploit them.

Aquarkiflus turn-ons include feet, confidence around geese, suggestive clouds, people who know when to applaud at both jazz and classical music performances, kites, snakes slithering over rocky terrain, the Ghost of Christmas Present, freshly bathed ferrets, ceiling fans, respecting boundaries, baseball pants, lumber, traffic circles, and Australian-rules football.

Aquarkiflus turnoffs include novelty ice cubes, chairs that look nice but are uncomfortable to sit in, escape rooms, beef breath, the word *moist*, the Ghosts of Christmas Past and Future, poorly packed luggage, pickup truck commercials, domineering tulips, spearmint gum, and anyone overly enthusiastic about celery (sure, it has its place, like in Creole cuisine or in a Bloody Mary, but there's never an occasion to be *thrilled* about celery, for heck's sake).

LOVE LIFE

In love, you're a humble square of dry dish rag. Though seemingly unglamorous, it is one of the most lovable and loving forms.

You're a dry rag, plunged into a sink of pure soapy love, until it saturates every fiber of your clothy being.

And you spread this love over everything you encounter: over the counters you encounter, the stove tops, the fridge doors that were smattered in lovelorn fingerprints. You cover them in your loving embrace. And when some cute dish comes to you, showing up at your sink, welcome them in for a plunge of (G-rated) liquid love smushings. You will scrub and be scrubbed, feeling renewed and awash in foamy adoration.

Yes, a humble dish rag can be such a loving form. Anytime you feel down or crusty, remember that you are not just lowly, you are a lowly rag, the epicenter of an ecosystem of loving affection revolving entirely around the wonderful crusty rag that is you.

HOW TO BE YOUR HAPPIEST AQUARKIFLUS

Some days you feel like those wind-up chattering novelty teeth, except you've been wound up to some unfathomable degree—a near-infinite wind—and you've been released on a glockenspiel to chatter away, creating a cacophonous clamor, unsure what horrible key this music is in, yet having no choice but to keep chattering away at it.

But look! You are not a wind-up toy. You can pause at any time. You can set down your squishy body and rest it—on a glockenspiel or elsewhere. You're a soft mound of muscles and guts, not plastic mechanical chattering teeth.

Somehow it can be hard to remember that you are the one in charge of your own life, not merely a pickleball ball plonked around by other people's paddles.

At any moment you could rest for ten seconds, and no one would notice. A slightly larger but worthwhile risk: Take a whole hour to just drift around like a beautiful balloon. You could pause your life, run out of the room, and go watch birds flutter through the sky, or whatever peaceful scene fits your mood.

You must find yourself a swath of leisure pursuits that bring you the purest pleasures and serve absolutely no productive function. Because these things truly matter, and absolutely do not chatter.

PISCERRS

Piscerrs

FEBRUARY 19 - MARCH 20

PISCERRS ESSENTIALS	
ELEMENT	Xenon
FLOWER/PLANT	A tall tree with thick foliage that gets a sudden dump of heavy snow and all its boughs bend dramatically, but they don't break, and soon the tree stands back up, tall and luscious
GEMSTONE	A piece of amber with a small lizard trapped inside
NICKNAMES	Spinning Fish, Doublefish, Fish Friend, Fishy Fishy Pudding Pants
ANIMAL	A pensive lemur, basking in the wind
DANCING STYLE	Jagged, erratic, like someone unskilled at charades acting out *chainsaw*

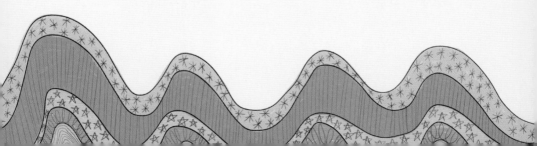

HOW TO SPOT A PISCERRS

Look out yonder just below the banana-colored sky, where water laps daintily at low-flying birds and waves dance with energy as boundless as the sun. Somewhere out there you'll find a Piscerrs, sprouting from the ocean floor, placed into a bubble of delicate sea foam, and sent into the world.

For this is how Piscerrs are made. They are snuck into human wombs via sea bubbles when they're two or three cells old (yet they are still fertilized by both human parents in a process that is as complicated as it is revolting, so let's not belabor it here). Consequently, they will always be genetically part sea-beast. And if you look closely, you can see this aquatic beastliness—the faintest hint of gills and a fin or two attempting to grow beneath their skin.

Quintessential Piscerrs Celeb

Every Piscerrs looks up to the "stylin', profilin', limousine riding, jet flying, kiss-stealing, wheelin' and dealin' son of a gun," professional wrestler Ric Flair. With a blond mullet and sequined robe, Flair played the "heel"—the naughty no-no boy—of wrestling for fifty years.

But all those whacks over the head with folding chairs nearly didn't happen. Three years into his career, Flair broke his back in a plane crash, and he was told he'd never piledrive again.

But a Piscerrs is never down for the count. In his words: "Diamonds are forever, and so is Ric Flair." It takes this fishy, Piscerrean strength to rebound from the oceanic depths of injury and hop back into your spandex onesie.

IDEAL CAREERS

Walker of Dogs, Tender of Bar, Grower of Kale, Mower of Lawns, Relaxer of Hair, Finesser of Details, Pickler of Pecks of Peppers, Pinner of Balls, Puller of Punches, Swatter of Flies, Spinner of Yarns, Dunker of Tanks, Getter of Goats, Spicer of Ham, Jiggler of Jam, Thrower of Pots, Tickler of Ivories, Humpter of Dumpties, Conjuror of Cheap Tricks

THE PISCERRS AT WORK

With a heave-ho and a ho-heave, and occasionally even a heavey-hidily-heavy-hoo, a Piscerrs will get down and dirty—or, if necessary, up and clean. A Piscerrs is not intimidated by the heavy heave-y tasks, regardless of direction or cleanliness.

They'll roll up their sleeves and their pant cuffs, and then they'll run out into the street, find a stranger, and roll up that person's sleeves too. And in this new state of up-rolled sleeves, the stranger will fall to their knees with deep Piscerrean inspiration and begin a spontaneous heave-ho, and a ho-heave, and then everyone around them will roll up their own sleeves and join in, and suddenly everyone is working together to heave and ho in a hoopla, until they're all hoarse with chutzpah. How heavenly to have the husky high of Piscerrs hysteria heaped healthily upon the hordes.

Such is the impact of a Piscerrs when they put their mind to their work. When they heave the hearts of those around them, a great ho is sure to follow.

HOW TO WOO A PISCERRS

Piscerrs can be a fickle fishy. One moment you think you've got them at the end of your line, and the next you realize you've caught a boot. But hope is never lost. Because you've got yourself a secret weapon.

And that's a bright, healthy selection of fresh fruits cut into snack-size pieces. Almost no Piscerrs can resist. And when you have lured them in with your mangoes and sliced pears, you can wow them with your effortless charm. You can regale them with clever anecdotes. You can ask them questions about their life and interests and perhaps discover that you both like British police procedurals. Then, all of a sudden, you're chatting about *Midsomer Murders*, discussing which of DCI Barnaby's sidekicks was best. And when you both agree it was Troy, the Piscerrs stops being so darn fickle, cocks their head to the side, smiles, and asks if you have any more of that ripe papaya.

LOVE LIFE

That scrumptious heart of yours—certainly it's a pitter-pat machine at the center of your circulatory system, but it's also a soft sugar cookie. And what you need is someone to decorate your cookie with a devoted dusting of sprinkles rather than gobbling it down like a stoner with the munchies.

It's a lot of trust to hand over your delicate cookie heart, so you don't do it for just any old bird. And you're perceptive—you can tell when a suitor has the hungry eyes, like they're just going to break off a piece and run away to eat it, giving you nothing in return. And if that happens, if someone does break your cookie heart and gobbles it up like some greedy, hungry jerk, know that you can always bake yourself a new one. It just takes a bit of patience, a bit of time, and a bit of all-purpose flour.

HOW TO BE YOUR HAPPIEST PISCERRS

If you are a Piscerrs, there is one pivotal key to inner splendor: You must keep an uncluttered mind. You must not be a mental hoarder. If you think some of your excess thoughts may be of value, then open up your brain garage and have a sale—slap prices on any ideas and concepts that may be desirable. Fifty cents for that stray fantasy about Richard Ayoade playing tennis on a surfboard—you can't be the only one interested in that. Six dollars for that box of concepts about non-potato Pringles. (Let's dig around that box for a second: Plantain Pringles, Freeze-Dried Marionberry Pringles, Prawn Pringles . . . wow, someone should really organize this box! Nah, just slap a sticker on it and sell it all!)

As for the thoughts that are of definitely no use to anyone—the nagging guilt, the horrid shame, the stabby-stabby anxiety about things that are definitely not going to happen—what about those? Well, you can thank those thoughts for coming out and for what they were attempting to do for you (they sincerely meant to help!) and then toss them in the nearest dumpster.

Keep your keepers and put them on a special mind shelf. Dust and polish them and give them precious mind kisses regularly. An uncluttered mind is a happy Piscerrs mind. And, may I say, a rather charming mind too.

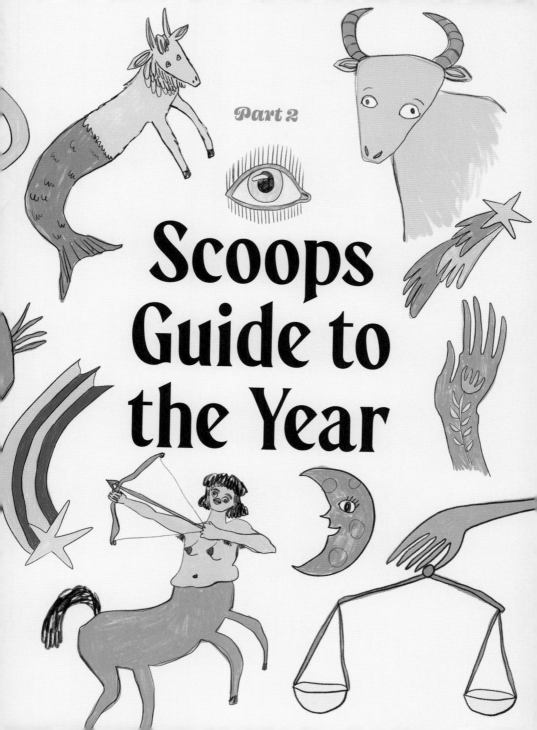

Part 2

Scoops
Guide to
the Year

JANUARY

January

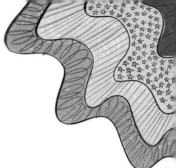

*A*h, January, that time of year when your body has crinkled up into a crispy cracker, a frosty crunch of beef jerky. It's now your job to soften and stretch it back out into its proper shape, whatever that is. Probably a vaguely human sort of shape? Do you recall having legs at some point? Did they once sprout from somewhere below your buttocks? How do we get them back? Let's explore.

If you remember only two words, let them be *limber* and *lotion*. Wiggle and bend and stretch that bod until limberness returns, then slather it up with your moistening agent of choice.

This is January success. A new year, a new start, a new corporeal form to slither into.

New Year's resolutions? Fine! If you must. It is natural to be curious about change and newness. Just be gentle to your sweet self, and whatever you do, don't endeavor to lose that beautiful tummy. Your tummy is a dear friend, a soft pot of comfort. It is a tender companion attached at all times to your middle, ready to be hugged and snugged at a moment's notice. It is a sacred thing to be celebrated any day, but especially on January 2, which is the day when all the celestial bits align in celebration of buoyant bubbling bellies.

January 20: Clopricrumb Season Out, Aquarkiflus Season In

Each year is clomped in with the steady hooves of our friend Clopricrumb. Our sweet baby Goat Fish is having the most special time, and wow, aren't we all just mushy swamps of delight on their behalf?

Dragging a massive fish tail behind them, they start our year full of hope, full of goat-eyed optimism, full of the dewy promise of new possibilities.

Cloppy season is a time for harmony between the goatiness and the fishiness within you. Stand firm on your rugged goat haunches, my sturdy and industrious love. And when you are through the firm times, you may melt into the wriggliest of fishes.

Then comes the start of Aquarkiflus season.

A full season of water dumpers, forever releasing their streams upon us like a river bursting through a dam built by an unskilled beaver.

But that endless flow is not you, my baby beetle bug! You're not a jug that can pour forever and will never empty. You have a bottom (and *what* a bottom!). You must make time to nestle into a cozy winter cocoon of splendid fuzz and to rest, even before that crinkly sweet body of yours feels noticeably weary. Be good to yourself during Aquarkiflus season, my peaceable plum. Treat the humanity in you like a precious baby hedgehog that was put in your care by a benevolent wizard who said, "No harm must ever come to this pure and lovely creature!"

That hedgehog is *you*.

Holidays in January

January 1 ***Cocoon Day:*** It's a magical day of renewal indeed! The longer you spend wrapped tight inside a makeshift cocoon, the more refreshed and renewed you will be when you exit, making for an even fresher start to the brand-new year and the newest of yous.

January 2 ***Blessed Belly Day:*** Today's the day for honoring your belly, be it big or small. Love your tum-tum, a magical friend of soothing delights, a glorious pot of blooming roses. Even if you somehow have a six-pack yourself (why?), soften your heart and soften yourself to the wonderfully wiggly-jiggly midriffs the world over. Hug your tum, and if you can kiss it, you are double blessed.

January 9 ***Tell Your Secrets to a Poodle Day:*** Find a trustworthy poodle (you'll know), and whisper to it your heart's hidden no-no's. All at once you will feel lighter and fluffier, as if your insides were as light as the very puff of a poodle's bounciest floof.

January 22 ***Day of Remembrance for Fallen Houseplants:*** A moment of silence, please, for our dearly departed friends. Oh, houseplants, we hardly knew ye. We tried! We tried. We sincerely, kind of, sort of tried.

January Journal Prompts

1. It's a new year according to the Gregorian calendar that we adopted in 1582 and have all just gone along with ever since. Describe in gooey details the many delicious things you would like to eat this year, and where you'd like to eat them, and who you'd like to eat them with (or off of). Set some big, tasty food goals.

2. If you could painlessly remove your butt and sell it for money, leaving you with a concave posterior, how much would you sell it for? What is a roundish rump really worth to you? Does it have a price? Could you cope with a junkless trunk?

3. In cold climates, the queen bumblebee hibernates all winter. The rest of her colony has died, and it's up to these fuzzy, plump gals to dig a hole in the ground and survive the long, cold season alone. But imagine they weren't just sleeping in their underground burrows. Imagine that they've dug their individual holes, and all of these big queens ended up together someplace . . . else. What is this place? What are the queen bees *really* doing all winter? Write what you imagine these thicc ladies are up to. Start writing, and see what comes out.

January Scoops

ARBYS

This marks your luckiest month for thrift shops, flea markets, and the like. While others rest their wallets at the beginning of the year, you scrape together some pretty pennies and prance to the secondhand ateliers.

When you enter all manner of junk shops and purveyors of used goods, you are a magnet for curiosities—be it the designer jeans with a $3.99 price tag, the enormous chameleon brooch you didn't know your life was missing, or the record you almost bought for full price online but found right there in the bargain bin. My gosh!

TORBUS

January is the time for celebrating your upper limbs—the soft noodles of flesh that protrude into jabby-stabby elbows, then climax into weird wrigglers that you call hands. What a splendid configuration of muscle and bone! What wondrous tasks these mechanical grabbers can perform! How strange it is to be an organic meat robot covered in porous skin!

In this most annum-beginning of months, stretch your limbs, honor and moisturize these darling danglers, tend to your nail beds, read your palms a story, and smooch those dexterous extremities in exactly thirty-eight spots each.

GERMINI THE TWRNNNS

It's cold outside, and the strip club is full for a Tuesday afternoon. A dancer emerges from a black curtain, illuminated by purple and blue spotlights, wearing a tiger-striped bodysuit and a blank expression. Her hands are hidden from view behind her back as she inches toward the shining silver pole. When she reaches the pole, she pauses. She tenses.

The dancer reveals why her hands were hidden: Behind her back she was holding a long, sharp butcher's knife.

Turning the knife in front of her face, she watches the colored spotlights reflect off the shiny, sharp metal. The men quiet down, uncertain, afraid.

The dancer in the tiger-striped bodysuit raises the knife slowly, then swings it down, and cuts straight through the solid silver stripper pole in front of her. The knife goes smoothly, softly through the pole. The crowd is stunned and confused. She cuts again, from a lower angle, and finally they understand: The pole is cake.

She removes a thick wedge of cake, holding it in her hand. The bite she takes is large and greedy. She smiles, enjoying it. She quickly devours the whole piece. The men are unsure how to react. Some consider leaving, but the plush booths and warm neon lights feel so cozy. The dancer takes another slice and relishes it as much as the first. The men start throwing her all the money in their wallets.

It's so cold outside. It's so comforting here. She's enjoying the cake. They're happy for her.

CONSUR

If you woke up one morning buried up to your neck in poisonous snakes instead of tucked safely in your sweet bed, could you keep your cool? Could you slowly, gently explain to the snakes that you needed some coffee or tea, or at the very least a few moments to wake up and consider things before anything wild happens? Could you patiently kiss each snake on its venomous left fang?

Luckily, it is fairly unlikely that you are going to wake up tomorrow covered in cobras and vipers and rattlers. I can all but guarantee it. I mean, you've made an enemy or two, and there's that one guy who has always been really into reptiles who has been holding a grudge for years. But the important thing to consider is your adaptability: keeping that cool little cool of yours, my Snippy Snipper. Can you keep your Consur claws from clipping reactively even when you're in the gravest of dangers?

LEMO

Your heart is a skyscraper, scratching at the sky, giving the sky one heck of a back scratch. And the sky is so very pleased to be so pleasantly scratched by the sweet claws of your heart that it has the sorts of gifts to bestow that only a vast expanse of endless space masquerading as a blue ceiling could give to a sweet and tender Lemo's heart. The sky this month will sprinkle your tall skyscraper heart with wondrous celestial clarity, the sort you've been longing for.

The trick is that you must sit very still, or you could miss it, or worse, you could mist it back up with your human brain mists. Sit still, examine your heart, and notice—wow! The sky really has bestowed a mystical clarity on your heart. You think, *I know exactly how I feel about goat cheese on fish dishes! I know my opinion on whether basketball shorts should be real short or real long! I have perfect clarity on the important issue of alfalfa sprouts in sandwiches!*

Use this heart clarity well.

VURBO

This month, you're like a cat on an obstacle course: capable but obstinate. You're completely unwilling to weave your way through all these ridiculous obstacles just because someone put them there. You need meaning. You need passion. You need belly rubs.

Dogs will run their tail-wagging way through an obstacle course just for the pure joy of movement, and that's absolutely a beautiful way to live. Sometimes you're in that tongue-out, wide-eyed mode of jumping through hoops for the pleasure of being in the air. But this month you're more cerebral. You want to know who put the hoop there, why they want you to jump through it, and maybe if there's a sunbeam you could nap in instead.

LEHBRAH

All the features of your face will fall off, and you'll have a perfectly smooth face for a while. You won't be able to see or smell; you won't talk or taste or hear. You'll have to venture inward, into your own silly mind. You will have to be comfortable presenting a face to the world that no one will recognize and that none of your loved ones will light up at.

It will be challenging, but one small mercy: Without eyes, you won't be able to see how ridiculous you look.

Best of all, it will only be for a few seconds here and there, and it will mostly be while you are pooping, so it won't be much of an inconvenience. It may even be an olfactory relief. Just make sure, if you wear glasses, to watch them closely, lest they slip off your occasionally smooth face while you do your bathroom business.

SLURPEEO

You *can* count your chickens before they hatch because you have exactly three, and they're starting to hatch right now. Their names are Ruth, Dolores, and Cybil, and when they finish hatching in a moment, they'll start out as chicks the size of minivans, and soon each will grow as large as a double-decker bus. They live only in your mind, but in there they are real, feathery, and magnificent.

These chickens are wonderful mental companions. They will be warm and kind to all your positive thoughts, and they will peck out the eyes of any wandering thought that tries to bully you. Seriously, it will be absolute poultry carnage to any mental unfriendlies.

If anyone in your real life is mean to you? The lingering bad feelings that would typically remain will get nibbled up by these three helpful hens, as if the hurt or resentment were a tasty handful of seeds and corn.

SPLATTITARIBUS

There's a beautiful, snowy hill in Austria, and one day in January every year, a thousand ripe melons suddenly roll down it, seemingly out of nowhere, toward a small village. They'll come one or two at first, and everyone in the village will yell, "Melons! The melons are coming!"

There was a time when the village built a wall to protect themselves from the speeding melons, and the melons smashed against the bricks, inedible. And who can blame the villagers? Imagine the damage a honeydew can do at full velocity! But then one day, a young girl hopped the wall while everyone watched in terror and caught three twirling winter melons in her fishing net. Her family made a delicious winter melon soup, big enough to share.

The villagers were inspired. They tore down the wall, and from then on they caught the melons, gently cradling their tumbling rolls, not fearing even the girthiest watermelon.

The point is this, my sweet Splatty Baby: What feels like a danger may actually be a sweet gift. Examine what scares you. That eeky twinge of fear may be nothing but a ripe, tumbling cantaloupe.

CLOPRICRUMB

You will spend thirteen minutes every day body-swapped with a total stranger, another Clopricrumb who leads a totally different life from your own. They're typically far away, across the planet, with different beliefs, values, bodies, thoughts, and experiences. One afternoon you'll be an elderly airboat captain in the Corroboree Billabong Wetlands of Australia's Northern Territory, then the next evening you'll be the lead on a recreational Dutch men's curling team, and one Tuesday morning you'll be a newborn infant in Ouagadougou, Burkina Faso (unless you already are a newborn infant in Burkina Faso, in which case, congratulations on your excellent reading skills and even more excellent taste in reading material).

Sadly, the body swaps are almost completely wiped from your memory. But if you stay present and alert throughout your day, you'll be a little more alert during the swaps, and a pinch more of the wisdom and experience from your visited bodies will stay with you when you swap back.

AQUARKIFLUS

You've been known to glow in the dark. Known by whom? Why, the hamburger people, of course.

The tiny anthropomorphic hamburger people, who parade through your bedroom at night while you sleep to put on a little show for the microscopic mites who live in your eyelashes. And trust me, your eyelash mites *love* these shows even more when the hamburger people are illuminated by you glowing in the dark.

Your eyelash mites all have their birthdays in January, and the hamburger people are planning a special show for the occasion. So even if you don't think you can control it, try extra hard to glow in the dark. Your kind efforts are appreciated by those around you.

PISCERRS

This is an incredibly denim time for you. You have your best looks and best lucks in wide swathes of denim, so embrace the hearty blue friend. If you've got a denim vest and hat to add to an outfit, or want to brave the winter in a denim parka, all the better! Watch your love life heat up to a simmering sizzle when you pair wide-legged denim trousers with denim boots. Feel your boss throw promotions your way as if they were the hottest of potatoes when you show up to a meeting in an all-white denim power suit.

(Note: Denim results may vary.)

February

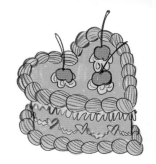

he Anglo-Saxons called February *Solmonath*, which translates roughly to "cake month," and boy were those Anglo-Saxons on to something.

Our own word for the month, *February*, comes from some Roman festival where people washed themselves. I'd much rather concentrate my efforts on eating mass quantities of cake to soothe my winter blues than spend all month reminded of how badly I need a shower (because, trust me, *I know*).

February is a short little sprite. She doesn't need all those extra days to get her monthiness done. She can manage in twenty-eight what others take thirty-one to do.

February: our deep, dark, brooding friend of a month. A month where we wedge compulsory Valentine romance halfway through to try to keep spirits, profits, and blood sugars high. Where even pizza restaurants awkwardly force their dough into heart shapes just to extract some strained and hollow sensations of sentimentality out of our limp and lifeless souls.

Oh, perhaps that's a tad cynical. February is full of cheeky quirks, like how we quadrennially plop an extra day into her because Pope Gregory XIII thought that'd be a nice place to stash it.

Truly, February is our manic pixie dream month. So perhaps, in this most strange of months, there's a way to have our cake and cleanse it too.

February 19: Aquarkiflus Season Out, Piscerrs Season In

Aquarkiflus season continues gushing through our lives with such luscious generosity, moistening our puckered lips as we num-num-num it up in little kitten laps. When Aquarkiflus season passes, our outsides may dry out, but our insides remain like a dewy swamp, squelching joyously from the liquids that remain.

The water-dumping energy that starts February off is a time to contemplate where we're dumping the waters within us. Be mindful: You have only so much dumping to dump. Cherish your dumps. Not everyone deserves your divine waters, my darling. Save your moisture, like the cutest camel.

Then we flop into the spinning fishes of Piscerrs season, forever smooching at each other's tails, forever twirling their fish dance in the sky.

We welcome these windmilling sea cuties, spiraling like flailing whirligigs of the oceans deep.

But this Piscerrs energy is not a wayward fish spinner. Their marine-copter has purpose, has direction, has dinner plans. And so, too, will you find yourself spinning toward destiny.

This is a time for intricate celebrations, homemade party hats, and tiny xylophones played with underripe eggplants. And all this spinning fish energy keeps flying in the background, slapping you in the neck with cold, damp caudal fins in a way that wakes you up, shakes you up, and reminds you that you are truly alive.

Holidays in February

February 7 ***Stick to Your Friends the Way Slightly Moist Frogs Stick to Each Other Day:*** Moist frogs are mildly adhesive and naturally want to stick together. Do this, either figuratively or literally, with your own human friendlies.

February 14 ***Revolt against Enforced Sentimentality Day:*** A day for deep skepticism against everything that seeks to artificially manipulate your sensitive heartstrings. Your emotions are sacred, and you won't let them get pinched and prickled by just any dollar-store ruffle or waxy chocolate. Not today, no ma'am. If smooches come with sincerity, then smooch those smooches. But if they are as contrived as a wonky factory-made cupid doll with half its stuffing missing and a plastic googly eye dangling off, then perhaps reconsider.

February 23 ***Take Better Care of Your Hygiene, You Absolute Slob Day:*** You've let yourself go. It's clear to anyone who sees you that you've stopped caring not just about your appearance but about the odors you allow your meaty flesh package to ooze. We're going to tidy that up, OK? Start with your breath, and work your way out.

February Journal Prompts

1. What if your legs were two miles long, and you couldn't stand, you just had to awkwardly shuffle around trying not to knock too much public property over between your torso and your feet while you did it, and you never knew which district to register to vote in because your body was never in one place at one time. How would you overcome the many trials and tribulations?

2. Cucumbers don't like you. They don't like your hair, they don't like your face, and they really don't like the way you talk. OK, that's not true; cucumbers are in fact quite neutral on the subject of you. But consider how their potential hostility made you feel.

3. Would you like Valentine's Day more or less if you were in charge of putting a large adhesive doily on everyone's face, and everyone just went with it and passively let you slap a giant frilly circle to their face, and all day you just got to go around smacking strangers in the face under the pretense of festive doily adherence and no one complained? Discuss.

February Scoops

ARBYS

Watch your eyebrows this month, for they will get hungry and attempt to escape your face in search of a feast. This may not sound serious, so lean in and hear this cautionary tale.

One February, an Arbys named Amanda was making a pot of gravy when her eyebrows escaped, leaping directly into the boiling pan. Amanda, aghast, ran to the bathroom to examine her smooth forehead. While she was away, her eyebrows sucked down every bit of gravy, growing strong, infusing themselves with thick, meaty power. And they were not done. They ravaged Amanda's kitchen, eating everything from her mixed nuts and artisanal flour to her entire refrigerator and stove.

The eyebrows grew and grew, and when Amanda returned, there was no kitchen left, just eyebrows devouring her entire 1960s bungalow. Amanda leapt out a window just as the eyebrows busted through her roof, throwing shingles all down her quiet suburban block.

Satisfied, her eyebrows longed to return home to Amanda's face, even though each hair on the massive brow-beasts was now as thick and long as a telephone pole. They approached Amanda, keen on reconciling, but seeing the gargantuan masses of brow atop the rubble of her abode, Amanda turned and ran. The brows wormed slowly after her. Amanda remains on the run from her own eyebrows, unsure of what will happen if they ever find her.

TORBUS

Hooray! February may feel like this cold, short month of misery, but for you, my dumpling Bullchild, it's a dazzling, icy escalator to success.

Whether you notice or not, simply by letting your body drift into the temporal reality of February, you're moving both forward and upward, as if you were on the escalator at the Mall of the Spiritual Plane. You're ascending, you're growing, you're evolving, and all you have to do is rest that precious Bullish body of yours. Let this spiritual escalator do all the heavy lifting.

Sure, of course, you can stroll upward and move along faster. If you feel the pep, then yep, step by step, give it a schlep. But if not, do not worry. Recline, get fully supine, drink some wine, it's fine! Save your strength for March, when all emotional and spiritual growth goes back to taking the stairs.

GERMINI THE TWRNNNS

Oh, what a fresh and brilliant month you are in for! Shurleen, the goddess of shower inspiration, showers you with extra blessings this month. You will leave your chamber of cleanliness not only well washed, but also bursting with creative innovation.

Shurleen is a generous goddess, plopping helpful ideas into our brains while we're zoned out mid-scrub. What a darling! And every February she sprinkles extra blessings upon sudsy Twrnnns. She'll scrub you with ingenious ideas, shampoo you with grand schemes, and loofah you with wild creativity.

Enjoy Shurleen's bounty! And keep something to scribble your ideas on nearby for when you bound out of the shower,

drenched with both water droplets and Shurleen's sweet gifts of inspiration.

CONSUR

You will be visited in your dreams by the love machine.

The love machine is a complex device that will put your subconscious through its paces, so giddy the heck up.

First it will inflate you to increase your buoyancy and rotundity (both helpful in love). It will suck your psychic body into its main machine, and you will be helpless to escape, so best to just relax and let the love in.

The love machine will wash any stale and crusty resentment off your internal organs and will paint on a fresh coat of love-flavored buttercream frosting. Then it will vibrate you at a frequency of 639 Hz to tenderize your human meats, which will be injected with a marinade of pure love and a splash of Dr Pepper for flavor. Finally, you will be wrapped in a burrito of soft love silks by a fleet of puffy, floating kittens blessed with eternal youth.

You will feel glorious, and whether your conscious mind remembers what your subconscious has been through or not, you will be changed: You will be forever lighter and ready to bring these feelings of freshly minted love to everyone you meet.

LEMO

Your broth game reaches its peak this month; you will be one with soup or any other brothy business you attempt. Even bathing and stewing in your own human-bathing broth will go wonderfully well for you.

So broth boldly, choose your flavors with conviction, and stir that soup with confidence. Heck, even allow yourself to dabble in the realm of arrogance. It's only soup! What harm does soup arrogance do? And how often do you let yourself trifle in the world of hubris? You spend so much of your life in your comfort zone of modesty and even self-effacement. Sure, that's so much more respectable, but it's so much less fun.

This is only broth, so broth with a blush of bluster. The scallions will understand. The aromatics aren't here to judge. Have a little fun with your formidable broth muscles in the land of Soupsville.

VURBO

Due to a cosmic whoopsie-daisy, there is an enormous elephant seal in the Patagonia region of southern Argentina that has a donut cannon (sort of like a T-shirt cannon at sporting events, except this one shoots freshly baked artisanal donuts).

This huge, husky creature wallops around a throne-like rock formation, shooting donuts at the other critters if they please her. And what pleases her? Musical theater, of course. Imagine all the seals and walruses and penguins along the shores of the Valdés Peninsula dancing and barking and squawking and getting donuts shot at their heads. It's a hoot!

Anyway, this month you can channel that energy, straight from the queen elephant seal (or Reina Elefante Marino, as she's known) herself. Even if you don't have a magic donut cannon, you can always buy a dozen pastries from your local bakery and chuck them at your friends' heads when they delight you.

LEHBRAH

The winter months are droopy and dreary, but you are in the home stretch, my lovely, lumpy Lehbrah! Celebrate, wriggle, and unfurl yourself as if you were your own red carpet.

The most important thing for getting yourself to the end of this wintery time is to ply your sweet cells with vitamins, love them with leafy greens, bless your beautiful baby body with many gorgeous vegetables, guzzle and glurg the good juices, and glug down a capsule of vitamins if you wish to augment your intake.

Cherish your darling body's resilience. You've endured the gloom of winter, whatever that has meant for you, my fluffy toughie, my sweet scaly Lehbrah.

SLURPEEO

What you're exploring this month is your buttery side, your puffed pastry side, your super silky creamy-but-tangy side, your French patisserie side. You're wondering, *Am I a little dainty petit four or a big bite of eclair? Have I been missing work lately because I'm a flaky little croissant? Have I always been so full of jam? Oui oui*, you think, *I'm a perfect profiterole.*

Turns out my sweet drizzle of confection perfection shining through the window of the patisserie, you're a pastry not meant for this planet, a platter of treats too perfect for this world. Just as some passerby notices you in the bakery window and thinks they could buy you up tart-by-tart, you blast off into the exosphere. You've become the first French patisserie in orbit, looking down on us with all that wisdom in your shining glaze.

SPLATTITARIBUS

Every February you start feeling a bit like a salamander bar, my sweet Splatty. What's a salamander bar? Well, some buffets have salad bars, and some have salamander bars, where a bunch of salamanders sit at barstools and order drinks at a miniature (but fully functional) bar set up behind a sneeze guard.

Salad bars provide a very real function at a buffet. Salamander bars are simply adorable. Februarys have you feeling like you lack the deeper utilitarian function of a salad bar, and all that remains is an absurd amphibian ordering a tiny martini.

It's natural to have these feelings. But you needn't worry. It turns out you are, in fact, a wonderful balance of salad bar *and* salamander bar. You're the best of both bar worlds, sneeze guard and all.

CLOPRICRUMB

You are so warm of heart in February that even when you feel the brittle chill so harsh you're worried the marrow in your bones may freeze solid—even then, there is something so warm at the soul of you that you must stay alert! Icicles melt when they sense you coming and may slip off rooftops. The skating rink may turn to a puddle under your feet. The hearts and minds of even crabby curmudgeons will soften curiously. It may seem like cold comfort that everything in your warm radius is melting when you're at the bus stop shivering. But if you can remember that extra pair of mittens, maybe some fuzzy earmuffs, and extra insulation anywhere you can stuff it, you may just be able to keep some of your own warmth in.

AQUARKIFLUS

Braces can move our teeth around—we're malleable creatures, if we're willing to go slow. We could make our teeth do anything with braces. We could make them all stick straight out like the prongs of a ceiling fan, as long as we are willing to give up chewing. And smooching, I suppose.

And if we could do that to our teeth, there is hope for anything we want to change: any aspects of ourselves we've been feeling bummery about. Brains are just our thinking teeth. They chew our thoughts. They don't want to move. They're stubborn, even painful when you start trying to get them to change.

That's why the best way to change is to make a habit; habits are braces for your brains. So figure out that change you want to make—reading more books, waking up earlier, or having ceiling fan teeth—and put on those braces.

PISCERRS

You are guarded every February by Jorgürn, the Norwegian spirit of cozy socks, fleece pants, finding everything on your list on quick shopping trips, and florid prophecies about brawny cave trolls who lob chunks of raw elk meat at their enemies to thwart the coming of the Pigeon Queen. That last one may have a little less to do with your immediate concerns, but nevertheless Jorgürn is a diligent spirit, and whether you need to remember toilet paper on your trip to the corner store or you need a husky troll to fling an elk thigh at one of the Pigeon Queen's orcs, you'll be cared for and blessed.

March

Spring is sproinging, my sprinkles of sprockets. As you bloom into this time of springing and sproinging, marvel at March! For March is the month of inner composting.

The tiny emotional red worms inside you are their most active, working to munch down your lifetime of humiliations (and there are plenty!), like that time you pooped your pants so badly at SeaWorld you had to abandon even your shoes in the bathroom, but your friends couldn't find pants in the gift shop, so you shuffled around for the rest of the day in a Shamu beach towel and dolphin flip-flops.

Yes, your emotional red worms are working hard to break down not just that joke trauma but your real traumas too.

Your emotional worms can do most of the work on their own. They need just one thing from you, and that is complete and utter validation of every emotion you dredge up. They can only compost it if you enthusiastically recognize that it is totally valid. Emotional composting requires immense self-compassion and hefty doses of fervent self-validation.

And soon you will have some fresh, nutrient-rich mind soil in which to plant whatever mental vegetation you wish.

March 21: Piscerrs Season Out, Arbys Season In

March begins with Piscerrs season, which endures with the energy of two calloused old sea captains, sheltering in the same lonely harbor one stormy night, their eyes meeting across the tavern, instantly admiring the cut of each other's jib, then spending the rest of the storm snuggled together by a roaring fire, sharing nautical stories and a few tender kisses, shaving a small dog, and ordering a large cheese pizza.

Piscerrs is a season of good hair, recipes working out the way you intended, and telling the woman at the post office she has a bit of lettuce in her teeth and her not making it weird at all. File your nails neatly and enjoy.

As the spinning fishes fly away, Arbys rams in gently with their Moog Model D synthesizer, a theremin, and a box of mysterious percussive instruments. Arbys season has composed an experimental electronic symphony based on the month of March and the whole concept of marching—knees up, in rhythm, as if we were guards parading around some old castle. But honestly, it sounds like Ravel's *Boléro* burped out by a computer.

Still, we applaud for Arbys season. It was an interesting performance, and we are happy they put themself out there and expressed their season in song form, even if this is a book and no one can hear it.

Holidays in March

March 4 ***Buttered Banana Day:*** Not for everyone, but if it's for you, oh boy!

March 7 ***Waddle Everywhere and Call Everyone Tim Day:*** Waddle like a little duck, and now everyone is named Tim. OK, Tim?

March 11 ***Thrift Shop as If It Were a Museum of Human Civilization Day:*** Honor every dejected piece of thrift shop bric-a-brac as if it were a revered relic of human achievement. The Celine Dion action figure? A part of our history. The creepy antique clown head that looks like it was painted by a color-blind Muppet on LSD? An important vestige of a bygone era. That piggy bank in the shape of a horrifying human baby with eyes that gouge so far into your being that they give your soul a colonoscopy? Why, it's simply a precious relic of 1990s craftsmanship that ought to be cherished forever.

March 27 ***Let a Toad Lick That Big Bone on the Outside of Your Ankle Day:*** Let a toad lick that big bone on the outside of your ankle.

March Journal Prompts

1. The majority of the Northern Hemisphere's foxes are born in March, making most of them Piscerrs and Arbys. How curious to have a whole species of animals that are mostly the same signs. They must get bored of having such similar personalities when they gather for their fox box socials. Reflect on a world where most humans are born in the same month and have the same signs. Would we look at astrology the same, or would the sky hold different mysteries?

2. In Helsinki, Finland, there is a Burger King equipped with a fully functional sauna. Yes, you can live every health inspector's dream and eat your Whopper in a steamy box of sweat. Maybe noshing french fries while you shvitz in public isn't your idea of a relaxing meal, but if not, what would be? Where would you eat, and what would you eat there?

3. If you were to wear some stunning formalwear—like a dashing tuxedo or an Oscars gown—made of butterscotch sauce, you'd look elegant and glistening, attractive to both humans and ants alike. But any chairs you sat upon would stick to you when you stood up. And none of your many admirers would hug you. Would this lack of physical body-smooshing be a positive or negative for you? How would you navigate the world in butterscotch formalwear?

March Scoops

ARBYS

What is it about this time of year, where Rammy Jammy jelly beans can't help but move their big booties around? Music is sucked into your spirit like a vacuum—a dance vacuum—and the spirit of dance is inside you.

But the spirit of dance is not without danger. You could twist so hard you wind up fusilli-shaped. Or you could shuffle so magnificently that a swarm of bumblebees fly into your home and cook you breakfast (the shuffle dance is perilously close to bee-speak for "a spinach and feta omelet, please").

So use caution as you wriggle your body rhythmically. Enjoy the shimmy-shakes within you, but tread softly within those dancing shoes.

TORBUS

If you started now, you could be the most muscular person in the world in a mere eight to ten years. You could be huge. A thick, sinewy giant. You could set records and enter those competitions where you pull buses further than the other muscly weirdos. Well, OK, it would depend upon your genetics and hormones, but you could be a big ole beast, with thighs like glistening hogs, a neck totally indiscernible from your jaw, and arms that look like a nylon sack of coconuts resting on your bewildering undulating torso.

Just, you know, think about it. Consider it. Don't completely count it out. Look in the mirror and visualize it. Maybe print out a picture of a hairless gorilla and paste your head on it just to get a visual.

GERMINI THE TWRNNNS

This month, my Doublesweet wonder, a new opportunity falls right into your lap. Unfortunately, this opportunity is soon eaten by a large kangaroo with an accountant in her pouch, who immediately starts trying to audit you.

The kangaroo hops around, following you wherever you go, giving you not one moment of peace. The accountant digs into the pouch and somehow pulls out every receipt you've ever thrown away, hounding you about every purchase you've ever made. No matter where you run, the accountant and the kangaroo are there, around every corner, behind every door, until you finally succumb.

The audit proves that you're not perfect, but pretty OK, especially considering the strange times we live in. When he's done, the accountant oozes out of the pouch and runs away without a word. You're relieved, until up pops a new, smaller accountant who had been underneath the whole time. You're wary, but this accountant doesn't care about your finances. They just want to hang out and watch TV and maybe go see that new art exhibit later, but also, if you're tired, no pressure; it's fully up to you.

CONSUR

Imagine, my Snippers, if all the world's cars were Ping-Pong tables on wheels, and instead of fuel all you had to do was find someone going to the same place as you and play Ping-Pong with them. The Ping-Pong tables would drive themselves, and we would provide the Ping-Pong power.

Pedestrians would have to watch for wayward Ping-Pong balls, public transportation would be a friendly tournament-style Ping-Pong track, and you might even leave an especially long bus ride with a small trophy. It would be a light bit of exercise, benefiting the reflexes, not to mention the delightful (dreadful?) social element.

What does this have to do with you? Well. You're a little like a Ping-Pong car.

Conceptually, you're brilliant. But you're not a fully formed idea yet. You're not quite practical for the real world. You're exciting and novel, but a little bit strange, and that's OK. In fact, it's much better. This is not a world you want to fit too well into.

LEMO

March for noble Kitteny Buns is a time of lyrical lapping. It's a time where sweet rhythmic words gently fall from your tongue and land in layers upon the paper before you.

In short, March is a month of poetry. Pretty blossoms of poems protrude from beneath your skull, and it's up to you to free them, with a wiggle of a pen, a twirl of the tongue, or a click-clack of a keyboard.

How to write a poem? Easy! Write a word. When that word is firmly in place, install another word next to it. Or below it. Nudge yet another word in somewhere new, and so on. If you're in an Emily Dickinson sort of mood, shove a few thousand dashes into the mix,

and you're done. It's easy. No one said the poems have to be good. Nothing you do in this life has to be good. "Good" is subjective anyway. You're a Lemo, after all! You're a wiggly, kitteny, liony thing. You decide what's good and what's even more splendid than that.

VURBO

Oh! You are in a custom sort of mood. The sort that could take an item from a shop, sure, but would be so much more pleased if you plastered your own imprint upon it. You'd like to paint a platypus on some jean shorts or stitch a little poem onto your knapsack.

I cannot tell you exactly the sort of project you will take on this month. The whole point is that bubbling up inside the bubbler inside of you is a long-held desire to make something your own. You're surrounded all day by objects; perhaps you've selected most of them, or perhaps not. But as you move through a world of objects, they start to shape you like the rocks around a river. And you'd like to shape them back a bit, with paint or glitter glue or a large blowtorch.

LEHBRAH

You've thoroughly repressed the memory of that time in your tweens when you squeezed a pimple and a fully grown miniature horse flew out of it and ran—startled and confused—around your bathroom, knocking everything off the counter and breaking your toothbrush holder.

You then dressed the miniature horse up in some of your clothing, as if he were your younger sibling, and took him on the bus to the edge of town. There you found a farm and asked the farmers kindly if they would call him Zits and give him a forever home, to which they reluctantly agreed.

But it's OK. You don't need to dredge up every little time you had a small horse burst from your face. It's enough to remember that your quirks are there for a reason: Every one of your so-called idiosyncrasies makes perfect logical sense—regardless of their relation to acne-embedded barnyard animals. You can go gently on yourself knowing that you're made up of a complex past that you have no control over now.

SLURPEEO

You are like a popular and attractive salmon swimming upstream—socially, everything is so easy, but the current you face is strong indeed.

All the other salmon see your value and adore you more than you realize. Maybe your fishy peers are too shy to even let on how popular you really are. Maybe your own self-confidence has been building so slowly you didn't even realize it. But here you are, a pinkish fish with a solid sense of self and a firm standing (or, rather, swimming) among your aquatic associates.

But the external struggles in your life remain—you are still in the middle of your fishy migratory season—even if socially you are as fluid and free as a popular and attractive salmon. Keep swimming, my sweet Stinging darling.

SPLATTITARIBUS

It's the sort of month where you take one look at our entire society and your being shouts, "No!"

You'd rather preform an interpretive dance in a pond for a couple of skeptical herons (knowing deep down that they approved).

And if society lured you back with promises of "money" and "housing" and "not freezing to death in your dancing pond," you'd go, but not without a lot of pouting and feeling ill at ease with the whole arrangement of having to live a squashed existence in order to get the necessities of life.

And so maybe you'll draw a picture of an approving heron and tattoo it to your shin, to remind you that you don't need to be in a pond to dance. And you'll hold on to your "No!" still resonating in your being, reminding you to move closer to ponds, to dancing, to a distant whisper of "yes."

CLOPRICRUMB

I regret to inform you that a large portion of your larynx wants to turn into a soft, salted pretzel. And although soft pretzels are wonderful treats, they do not make for a functional windpipe. The only way to prevent this from happening is to write a short poem (either rhyming or open verse is fine) about why you enjoy breathing. Recite this poem to your larynx aloud, using large, hefty inhales to power your vocal cords, reminding your whole throat how wonderful it is to breathe, to have breath, to speak, and to not fall over as an inanimate meat sack simply because an integral part of your anatomy got the whimsical idea to turn into a delicious snack.

AQUARKIFLUS

There's no easy way to break this to you, my dearest Dumper of the Waters. You're going to find yourself in some wildly awkward situations this month.

You might wave to a friend only to realize that not only wasn't it your friend that you were waving at but also it wasn't even a person. You were waving at a stack of lemons at the grocery store. You're not friends with those lemons. You haven't even introduced yourself to those lemons, let alone put in the months of effort it takes to build a real and intimate sense of friendship—yet, anyway. Maybe someday.

All you can do this month is roll with the punches, roll with the kicks, roll with any kind of jibby jabs that come your way. Before you know it, your shreds of grace will return, and you'll feel like your normal only partially awkward self.

PISCERRS

It is imperative that you invent definitions to the following words: (1) brainbobbery, (2) puv, (3) frogfondle, (4) jeff, and (5) squork. The stars are very clear that your brain waves desire the bending and flexing provided by this squorking exercise.

And before you think, *But what will I do next year? I will have already defined these words!* you can stop right there. Next year you'll be brand-new, and your brand-new brain will find all new definitions. So halt that brainbobbery right now.

April

pril froths in like a jellyfish on the way to a business meeting—a jellyfish whose briefcase keeps slipping through its long, undulating tentacles, who has already lost its necktie to the gyres of the ocean, who has an important deal to negotiate but can't find a subaqueous Starbucks at which to acquire a Triple-Shot Americano to absorb through the opening that acts as both its mouth and its anus. And then, when the jellyfish finally arrives and can, at last, set down its briefcase on a stretch of placid reef and collect its non-thoughts within its total lack of brains, it realizes that it's not a businessperson at all, just a joyous jellyfish. There is no deal, there is nothing to negotiate, and the briefcase is filled with a small snailfish named Rebecca. That's when April settles, and the jellyfish sees that gosh, there's the sub-aqueous Starbucks right there, and thinks, *I suppose I'll treat myself to a Crab Frappuccino with an extra shot of plankton. I mean, I swam all this way. I deserve it.*

Back on the dry, terrestrial parts of the planet, in the springtime regions of the Northern Hemisphere, a flower sprouts here and there, and the world becomes a place of keen greenery. And—as anyone with allergies can tell you—this budding gets right inside our bodies and blooms within us. So get your own body outside, leap and frolic, and let the leafy, flowery bits of the world inside you.

April 20: Arbys Season Out, Torbus Season In

Arbys season has squeezed us—not like a pimple (we do not ooze) but more like an accordion. We regale the eardrums of all within reach with a vibrant polka that exudes from our very spirit as the bellows of our being is compressed by this hearty season. Within this squeezing we have felt the warmth, felt the tenderness, felt the Raminess penetrate our souls. But no polka lasts forever—even the most effulgent tune must puff out its last breath—and our peppy, dancing, squeezing time folds to a close.

But fret not! As one horned beastie exits, another stomps in to take its place.

Torbus energy can be tricky. You see this creature and think Bully time will be staunchly stern, firm like the loins of masculine bovine, hefty as the haunches of a he-cow. One look at the confident brow of our Torbus friends and you think, *Wow, there is a serious person full of serious business to be taken seriously.* But lo! How wrong you are! Torbi are wiggly silly Billys, with hooves as light and fluffy as cirrus clouds, flying high in the troposphere, wispy and untethered to earthly burdens.

And that's what Torbus season beckons you to do. Untether, toss aside your serious grown-up concerns, and replace it all with maximum fluffiness.

Holidays in April

April 9 *Pretend You're a Beautiful Creature Made of Silk and Slime from the Shores of Slimetown Day:* I don't make the rules. Get on with it.

April 15 *Actually Start a Project You've Been Thinking about for a Long Time Even Though You Know It Will Never Be as Good as It Is in Your Head Day:* It hurts that nothing you do will ever be the perfect masterpiece it is in your mind. Heck, you should see how much better this very book was in my head! It was *so* cool and clever, and all your existential woes melted away just from holding it, and it smelled of lavender and levitated and played beautiful music and could project holograms of the entire universe into your eyeballs. Imagine that! But alas, I wrote this book instead because that's what my feeble, imperfect mind was capable of. But I'm glad I did this instead of nothing. And I hope you do your thing instead of nothing too.

April 24 *Tell Everyone You Got a Tattoo of a Gorilla Riding a Tractor over a Series of Tiny, Helpless Snails Just to See What They Say about It Day:* Will they be into it? Will they be mortified? You'll find out soon!

April Journal Prompts

1. Three dolphins want you to join their friend group. They have let you know through a series of affectionate high-pitched noises. Describe the best-case scenario that dolphin friendship could bring.

2. If you were a raccoon that somehow won the hearts and minds of your country and were just democratically elected its leader, what would your top five priorities be? (Remember, you're a racoon but also yourself and also a world leader. But again, very much a raccoon.)

3. One day you are going to die, and it is probably going to be both painful and terrifying. We don't much like to think about it, but it's the price of admission for getting to be alive and do all the fun things we get to do while we're here. It's like a fun vacation where we pay the fee at the end. The more we remember our inevitable death, the more we remember to enjoy the beauty around us—our lovely friends, the simple pleasures, our fuzzy pets, and everything else we're grateful for. (What, you were expecting this to turn into something surreal, even zany? Mortality isn't wild enough for you?) Discuss!

April Scoops

ARBYS

A wonderful new friendship is out there, just waiting for you to find it, but you've got to get out there and look! Where could it be? Is it behind the bleachers at the running track scouring for objects spectators dropped? Is your potential friendship in a canoe paddling in slow, lonely circles in an artificial suburban lake? Perhaps, perhaps, but you'll never know until you put yourself in a position to find out. And once you're out there, once you're your own human bait at the end of a friendship fishing rod, you'll know your friendship fish the moment you spot it. It'll be a found friend at first sight.

TORBUS

This month, you're like a shining falcon with golden feathers who plucks just one feather and leaves it on the doorstep of a depressed moth for her to find, and the depressed moth sees the rare and beautiful gift and is cheered up, if only a little. And you, as a glorious falcon, need no thanks from the moth. You know what you've done and what your feathery gift meant. You simply watch the moth flutter in circles around your bright feather as you glide away, wondering what other noble deeds you might do. You let out a cry and hear your own wild voice echo through the mountains, and all who hear it know that some majestic being must be nearby in the wide skies above.

GERMINI THE TWRNNNS

When you plant a garden, you're not just growing food; you're also growing a sense of peace within you from time spent outdoors, with your fingers in the soil, tending to something slow and quiet.

That is, until a family of vindictive gophers comes and digs up your garden from underneath, eating your seeds, snapping your precious baby seedlings, until all that is left of your garden is greenish carnage sprawled before your teary eyes and a trail of gopher holes that you swear look jubilant, even victorious.

And when this happens, my darling Doublesweet Twrnnns, there is not much left to do. You can curse the name of all gophers, or you can clean up your garden, start fresh, plant it again seed by seed, and begin a new bewildering journey of gopher proofing.

CONSUR

Hark! In this springy time, the birds move to and fro, returning from long voyages, flapping their way to new shores. Some travel so high you couldn't even spot their feathery bods, and some glide so well they manage a brief power nap mid-flight.

And you, you feel a twinge of this migratory call too. A call to roam flaps in your heart, urging you to waft on the wind as if your whole being were naught but a puff of steam. And perhaps you are!

Treat your steamy self. Let your body and mind go a-wandering. Whether it's a full avian migration or a few pleasant flutters around a local park, your internal warbler or goose will be oh so gleeful.

LEMO

There was a time only a few decades ago when every April, every three hours on the hour, every Lemo would get five gallons of whipped cream dumped on their head.

April was a challenging month for Lemos everywhere.

But one brave Lemo named Yukiyo Atsumi, who lived by the sea in Oga, Japan, loved it. She delighted in the whipped cream. It made her feel happy and sticky and alive.

One day, knowing how miserable the creamy dumps made everyone else, Yukiyo disappeared with a boat full of supplies and was never seen or heard from again. The whipped cream dumps stopped that same April. Here's what happened.

Yukiyo rowed out from the Oga Marina, then turned into the Sea of Japan. She found a large, uncharted island, an island hidden from our earthly radar, and she docked her boat.

There she built an elaborate structure involving metal rods, magnets, and—some say—ancient mystical symbols. Whether by physics or witchcraft, her structure manages to divert the entire Lemo whipped cream dump directly onto her. That's nearly three billion gallons of whipped cream every three hours all April. One wonders if she still enjoys it.

Yukiyo would now be seventy-nine years old. Will the whipped cream dumps return after she dies? Or will her structure endure? Only time will tell.

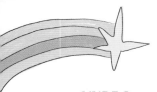

VURBO

Knock knock You wonder, *Who could be knocking at the door of my month?* You open it, and it's a wee angel. So, you let her in.

But oh dear! Turns out this angel is a pyromaniac, and she's setting fire to all sorts of things in your life: your fashion sense, that part of you that (mostly) grew out of picking your nose, and that little voice that keeps you from singing in public.

Oh no. The angel has torched many of your inhibitions and anxieties. Not your bad anxieties, I'm afraid, just the helpful ones that stop you from running out into traffic. You still have your common sense at least—wait, nope, that's gone up in flames too.

Well, it's going to be an interesting month. Good luck out there!

LEHBRAH

An old lighthouse keeper named Gentle Gilbert learned the secret of the photons. He learned that if he was quick, he could send messages out with his light beams.

Sailors would be surprised when, near the lighthouse, they'd hear Gentle Gilbert's whispered confessions: How he made himself friends out of fish sticks. Or that dancing alone to Taylor Swift made him happy. Or that he was thinking about getting a cat.

Eventually, Gentle Gilbert stopped sending his secrets. He felt silly, and a little embarrassed. Surely the serious sailors on those distant boats didn't want to hear his nutty ramblings. So he went back to his simple life, keeping the lighthouse, eating his fish stick friends, dancing to pop music, and he was all right.

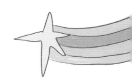

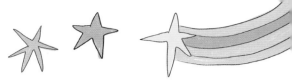

One evening there was a knock at the lighthouse door, and Gentle Gilbert descended the lonely stairs to see who it could be. He opened the door, and there were a hundred sailors, all carrying gifts. Some had boxes of fish sticks. Some had made mixtapes of their own favorite pop music. He had trouble seeing these beautiful gifts through the tears in his eyes. The sailors were grateful for the sweet messages that lighted their way through the dark nights at sea. As he let them in, up the stairs, he noticed one last gift. One sailor held an incredibly affectionate tabby cat named Paulina, who happened to be a fish stick–loving Swiftie herself. Gentle Gilbert's nights would never be lonely again.

SLURPEEO

If you were a tree, what sort of tree would you be? An aged oak or a plucky young apple tree just beginning to produce tart fruits for the picking? Would you grow weary and bored with the humdrummings of tree life, bored of the hopping birds, blind and bound in bark, finding it tedious to feel your roots in the same bit of soil day after day?

It is a month for such sapling contemplations. Put your feet together and your arms out, wave your body in the breeze as if you were a tree with bountiful boughs, and then separate your legged limbs and wander about once more, grateful that you are not.

SPLATTITARIBUS

My sweet Splatty dumpling, there's a wee flag flying—not quite a red flag, maybe a baby pink flag. It's here to warn you of the pretty

peacocks in your life. The elegant prancers who are delightful to look at, who bob their necks like the cocks of the walks, who floof out their grand tails and act as if they woke up like that.

These folks are a marvel for your ocular organs. But if you're not careful, the pretty peacocks in your life could snatch something special from you. That is to say, if you give in to their powerful orbit, a little of your own magic could get lost along the way.

So watch yourself around the peacock people. Keep your footing. And heck, floof out your own pretty tail, my sweet Splatty, you've got some pretty feathers of your own.

CLOPRICRUMB

Before the Earth was all filled up with liquid water, one of the gods (an obscure but pleasant one named Hamblorg, god of staying in your pajamas all day) used the dry ocean beds as a big bowl for mixing cake batter. Then he'd bake the cake in the sun's corona and mix several different colors of frosting in the Great Lakes, and when the fancy cosmic cake was done, he'd throw a little soirée in the heavens.

For you, April brings back the spirit of Hamblorg and this epoch. It's a month of repurposing, of finding new uses for all manner of odd objects. And—very important—this is also a time for making (or purchasing) and eating large quantities of cake, preferably in your pajamas.

AQUARKIFLUS

You're a cheerleader, your hands are living pompoms, and all the world is yours to pep. What you're leading the cheer for is totally up to you, but for April, you have a contagious amount of pep in your step, and you're entirely immune to those who would try to un-pep you. No one in your radius can resist the energy and ebullience you squirt around everywhere you go, even when you don't realize you're squirting.

So high kick! Body pyramid thing! Pike jump maybe! Gimmie an *A*! Gimmie a *Q*! What would that eventually spell? *Aquarkiflus!* Hooray!

PISCERRS

Look at the cobwebs! The dust! The little piles of junk you said you'd deal with but are still clumped in clusters of clutter, causing complete disarray inside your psyche. Yes, I do believe it's time for psychological spring cleaning.

Open the curtains wide in your brain attic. You're going to go through all those old boxes of useless childhood memories, the ones that you're holding on to because they reinforce outdated stories you've been clinging to.

Let's dig around a bit, shall we?

Well, howdy, it's a memory of that time you tinkled yourself on a childhood pony ride, which caused you to swear off all horseback riding, western films, and orange soda (the beverage that filled your bladder so full to begin with).

I think we can trash most of this? Or at least donate it to a charity. Maybe some hipster will want these memories ironically. But this is a month to reconsider making your current life smaller based on the things that happened to you in the past. Don't write off ponies because of a little past pee. Get back in the saddle.

May

Have you ever seen such a month as May? The flowers are really just showing off at this point, and you can barely step out the door without catching birds or squirrels copulating with reverent enthusiasm.

May is so utterly obnoxious with life and beauty and flourishing that it can overwhelm the senses if you're not prepared. You may want to keep a large cream pie in your nondominant hand for the duration, so if it all gets to be too much, you can pie yourself in the face, plugging your face holes with a thick custard and subduing the scene for a while.

But if you can tolerate it, May is the correct moment for a daring adventure known as a MayQuest.

A MayQuest is an adventure you take either alone or with select companions in—as you may have guessed—May. You pack a sack, stuff it with whichever snacks bring you the most delight and the clothes you feel the most gorgeous and confident in regardless of how much sense they make to the sensibilities of any other living being, and then depart for somewhere that seems like a lot of deeply pointless fun. Whether it's a day trip twenty minutes from your home or a three-week excursion across an ocean, it doesn't matter, as long as you can get up to some absolute nonsense.

May 21: Torbus Season Out, Germini the Twrnnns Season In

Well, look at that! Torbus season is still here, bulling around like a large Mancow. This Bullish Babe energy has been running through our lives, giving us a thick and meaty strength. And what shall we do during this time of muscular loins and pointy horns and large balls of fervor?

Why, only the goodest of deeds, the kindest of acts, the most gracious of gestures.

See a snail trying to lug a large cabbage across the street? Carry it for them! Or, better yet, explain to the snail why it absolutely does not need such a large cabbage. Just one small leaf would do. If the snail won't listen to reason, simply steal the cabbage from it. Tear off a small strip for the snail before you go, but don't listen to the snail's protestations. You're doing it a favor. The cabbage was only holding it back. You've done a good deed, and you can go home and have cabbage rolls for dinner.

After Torbus season, in dances the Twrnnns, two delightful darlings, arm in arm and doubly sweet. You'll be tempted to double up on everything, so watch out!

Play piano duets, order double scoops, play Double Jeopardy, make double entendres, lick your double honeydew melons, go tandem skydiving, and get your license to drive a double-decker bus. Just remain intentional about your duality, and watch the double dipping.

Holidays in May

May 2 *Yelling Day:* Shhh! Speak in a low, soft hush, barely above a whisper. Just kidding! Yell!!!

May 3 *Toga Yoga Day:* Do some yoga in a toga, as a beautiful blending of ancient cultures. And yes, collapsing in a bedsheet in corpse pose absolutely counts.

May 26 *Waffles Are Hats Now Day:* See a waffle? It goes on your head now.

May 31 *Bring Fresh Fruit to Your Mother Day:* The other "Mother's Day" is fine if you like commercial holidays invented by greeting card companies for profit. But what your mother really wants is a mango, and she wants it today. She also wants to see you and squeeze various bits of both you and the fruit. If you've lost your mom, eat some fruit in her honor. If your mom isn't great and doesn't deserve fresh fruit, substitute a more pleasant matriarchal figure.

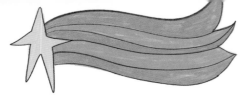

May Journal Prompts

1. Think of the last meal you ate in a restaurant. Close your eyes and relive the experience: who you were with, what the restaurant smelled like, the menu's font, your server's hairstyle. Recall the food itself: how it was plated, how it tasted, how it satisfied your beauteous belly. Add in all the other factors: the cost of the meal, your mood, if any fights broke out in the restaurant, whether you accidentally fell into a space-time rift and the hostess was too busy scrolling her phone to help pull you out of the alternate dimension you were slowly sucked into . . . stuff like that. Then write a full review as if you were a restaurant critic.

2. Think of the worst movie you've watched recently. Contemplate the casting, the script, and the cinematography. Try to think about why it failed so horribly, what was lacking, and whether a few more million dollars on explosions and CGI dinosaurs would have helped. Write a serious film review about this disaster.

3. What in heaven's name are you wearing? You call those clothes? Tear your own outfit to metaphoric shreds—lovingly, cheekily, but scathingly—in a fashion review for the ages.

May Scoops

ARBYS

This is your sour month, my Arbys Jammy Rammies: a month to savor tartness, to pucker your lips and suck in your cheeks until you're good and giggling. But it's not only sourness of flavor. Embrace the sourness of life and the sour side of yourself. Sourness is an underrated trait! How many dinners are made tastier with a zippy tang of lemon or lime? So dang many! Explore where you can add that punchy acidic bite to your own self, your own world, your own persona. Add tartness to a dance move, a curdle of fresh squeezed lemon over your handwriting, and even a tablespoon of apple cider vinegar to your love life.

TORBUS

If all the fish at a small, privately owned, but fairly well-stocked, aquarium were to suddenly find themselves stuffed inside your hand-crocheted Maud Lewis sweater—which you just finished that morning, with a charming scene of Maude's cats upon it—and this sweater were to urgently express how overextended it was feeling, elastically speaking, where would this leave you?

Well, waddling toward the nearest water source, I suppose, assuming you want this varied sea *life* to not soon become sea *death*.

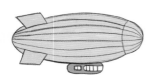

This is the sort of nonsensical situation you better prepare yourself for this month. Because you're going to need to know the answer to this question and other ridiculous tests of your morals, your cunning, and the stretchiness of your moss stitch.

GERMINI THE TWRNNNS

You feel untethered, like a blimp with a narcoleptic pilot. It's not easy to retrieve a sense of connection when you're fluttering away like a kite recently severed from its string or a go-kart that jumps the track, flying right out of the go-karting facility, through the parking lot, off the property, and down the shoulder of the highway for two or three miles, and then veers directly into the dusty wilderness, never to be seen or heard from again.

Begin the process of retethering slowly. Don't rush. Ground yourself in simple reminders of what you know for sure. Do you like potato chips? Yes? Then find a chip, cherish the chip, spend time with the chip, ingest the chip. No? Then substitute something you do like.

Reach out to those humans whom you feel the safest around, who would never swat away the feeble gesture of your extended hand. Let them know of your blimp-like state, of your narcoleptic pilot, of your go-kart in the dusty wilderness. Certainly they will understand. Certainly they will extend their own feeble limb, and you can connect, beginning to feel, at last, a tether.

CONSUR

Everywhere you go, you are the sprinkles on the cupcake, the teaspoon of cinnamon in the muffin, the dash of MSG in the phở, the reverb on the vocals, the glued macaroni on the kids' craft, the fresh strawberries on the oatmeal, the tahini in the hummus, the titanium in the alloy, the ginger ale in the punch, the surprise celeb cameo in the film, the 10 percent spandex in the fabric blend. You're that extra drizzle of drazzle. You give it the punch, the zhuzh, the stretch, the strength, the splash. Everywhere you go, whether you realize it or not, everyone is instantly brighter the moment you're around.

LEMO

Large segments of your brain turn into a substance not dissimilar to Jell-O this month. It's in there just wiggle-waggling all around, and if you were to shine a light on it, it would glitter magnificently as it went jiggledy-wiggledy like a luminescent alien creature.

This Jell-O brain can't think like a normal brain. You may struggle with basic arithmetic or fail to remember which animal goes "moo." You may try to use a fork for your soup and a spoon for your salad. But Jell-O brains have other advantages. Your dance moves will suddenly be wildly inventive and unmatched in their dynamism. You will look at your same old closet and concoct fabulous new outfits. Thrilling and bombastic words will slither into your everyday speech as if your teeth were made of carrots. And even your walk will take on a rousing new gait that pleases your shoes deeply.

Do not panic. Focus on the thrilling things you *can* do with this wonderful new brain of yours rather than all the bits of sadness that bubble up when you lament over the clarity you've lost.

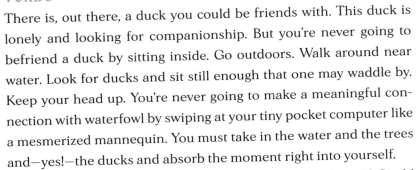

VURBO

There is, out there, a duck you could be friends with. This duck is lonely and looking for companionship. But you're never going to befriend a duck by sitting inside. Go outdoors. Walk around near water. Look for ducks and sit still enough that one may waddle by. Keep your head up. You're never going to make a meaningful connection with waterfowl by swiping at your tiny pocket computer like a mesmerized mannequin. You must take in the water and the trees and—yes!—the ducks and absorb the moment right into yourself.

When a duck waddles by, ask it, "Are you my friend? Could we be bosom buddies? Y/N?"

And let the duck waddle away if it's not to be. But don't give up! It's a big world, and there are a lot of ducks. You may never find your duck. But you've got to try. The journey to duck friendship is almost (almost!) as rewarding as the destination. The destination is duck friendship, though, so in this case, the destination (or ducksti-nation) is, indeed, a bit better than the journey.

LEHBRAH

You, my sugary, scaly Lehbrah, have style. You've got a prickle of pizzazz.

Your face is so captivating that—upon perceiving you—the eyeballs of other humans stop time, plop out of their human, join a mariachi band, and play a myriad of joyful songs until they become restless and discontented because deep down they love being eye-balls, so they'll quit the mariachi band, pop back into their human, and then restart the normal progression of time on the planet. Needless to say, this human will feel odd around their eyeballs and will blink repeatedly, not quite knowing why, and you'll often wonder, *Jeepers, why are everyone's eyes so dry?* but not really think too much of it.

All this is to say: You have pizzazz.

SLURPEEO

Imagine if, instead of being a dog walker, you showed up at someone's house and they handed you a thousand leashes, each as thin as a strand of hair, and each tied to a single grasshopper.

And they said, "Thank you for walking my grasshoppers," and you said, "No problem, this is my job. I'm a grasshopper walker," and you both wondered for a moment why you weren't called a grasshopper *hopper.*

Then you walked around trying to wrangle a thousand grasshoppers, trying to get them all to hop in a fairly uniform direction.

The whole task sounds like a bit of chaos. But you're no stranger to chaos, and you're no stranger to a challenge, either. This month will hold a challenge or two, but nothing that you and your thousand imaginary grasshoppers can't overcome.

SPLATTITARIBUS

Are there flowers falling down from the sky all around you? Are there little birds flying around and singing a song just for you? Are peanuts popping open and offering their nutty treats to you (unless you're allergic, in which case they're popping closed and bouncing far, far away)? Are trinkety treasures lolling around sweet shops simply for you to stumble upon?

I think perhaps all these gentle delights are grazing your life, softly tickling the tendrils of the fate that guides your journey on this mortal coil. So enjoy this month of tiny, precious miracles. And with each one that lavishes itself upon your lap, whisper a brief "Thank you" out into the vast mysteriousness of the universe, just in case there is a mystical newt or two listening.

CLOPRICRUMB

You're blessed! This month you have four guardian angels.

One is called Petey. He barfs out a full pool noodle every 6.24 minutes. So that's helpful.

The second is Slippery Sharon, the angel of sturdy foot-wear. (No idea how she received her moniker.)

Third is Archangel Tío Carlos, the angel of calisthenics, deep lunges, burning buns, and proper push-ups. Don't you dare put your knees over your toes while squatting this month—butt back! Tío Carlos is watching!

And last is Phil, who attracts small fluffy bunnies to you. (Drive carefully!)

It's a ragtag crew, but they're here for you. Call on them, even if your quandary is out of their purview. They will do their darndest to help—or will at least send a pair of ergonomic shoes and a pile of pool noodles.

AQUARKIFLUS

There's a small chance your skin could fall right off your body this month, so you may want to build a temporary backup skin suit, just to be safe.

Many different substances would be suitable for a skin suit (skin-suitable).

You could make a giant pot of sticky sushi rice and mold it to the shape of your body. Then if your skin falls off, you just slip right into your sticky rice suit and wear that around for a few days as your epidermis grows back. You'll look bright and puffy, and if you happen to get peckish and have a few grains for a snack, what's the harm?

Or if you're feeling a bit fancier and don't mind leaving a trail of leaves, dry some flowers and make a full-body dried flower bouquet. You'll be practically begging your skin to slip off so you can crunch around like walking potpourri.

PISCERRS

Just before the big bang, everyone in the world was crunched together more closely than any matter in the current universe, squashed into one singular point of infinite density—and that includes all of our armpits and nose hairs and butt cheeks. This is the kind of thought that makes it hard to look your barista in the eye. But that was 13.8 billion years ago, and this is now, and it's a good time to cherish the distance that now exists between your face and all the armpits and butt cheeks in the world. You can keep all your own bits fairly far away from other people's cracks and crannies, and if that isn't a reason to celebrate, then I don't know what is.

June

une is a fresh and aqueous time. It's a season to set sail, paddle, or put-put into some mass of water in a boat. If you don't own a boat, then build a boat, find a boat, summon a boat from an alternate dimension, or become a pirate and commandeer a boat (but not a super naughty pirate who murders and pillages—just a somewhat forward pirate who asks politely and uses a pleasant smile and a tip of the cap to convince some rubber-armed yuppie to lend out their kayak for an hour or two). Arr!

Back on dry land, June is a time for bequeathing names on all the entities and objects you hold most dear. People and pets aren't the only perky peeps who enjoy an auditory epithet. Your favorite sweater needs a name, your sourdough starter must have a moniker, your trustiest pants deserve a designation, and your car requires a sobriquet.

Names transform objects. Sure, Shakespeare wrote that "a rose by any other name would smell as sweet," but he put it in the mouth of Juliet, a lovesick teenager who was trying to hit on Leonardo DiCaprio. And who among us hasn't said something ridiculous when talking to Leo? The truth is, whether you name your couch Professor Smooth or Professor Concrete Aggregate, it'll change how you feel about your sofa. And if we called roses Instant Diarrhea Givers, they might actually smell a little less sweet.

June 21: Germini the Twrnnns Season Out, Consur Season In

During the first part of June, a curious energy splashes into you, rising and falling inside you like a tide throughout Twrnnn season. Think of it like TwrnnnNNNnnnNNNnnnNNNnnn season, as it ebbs and flows within.

Some days it's as if you have this extra burst of creative energy, the energy of a whole new person (your very own inner creative Twrnnn!) prodding you from within, tugging on your sleeve like a toddler. It's up to you whether you'll give in and let yourself play with pencils or paint or penning a tune. But your inner Twrnnn sure hopes you do before the creative tide rolls out again.

Then Consur season scoots on in, and we welcome the Snippy Snipper energy. Is the Consur going this way? Oh no, now the Consur is going that way. The way they zig and zag, these frisky friends will keep you on your toes. Which is exactly where you want to be this time of year: teetering on the tops of your toes. Teetering and twinkling around like the fingertips of a typist. Nimble, prepared, prancing, ready for anything.

In this crabby shell of hard chitin, we are safe to feel our crabbiest. We have the natural protection of Consur's carapace to let our crustiest long-suppressed emotions crabwalk to the surface and exorcise themselves out of our inner trenches and into the ocean's depths, never to return.

Holidays in June

June 1 ***Buy a Drummer a Bagel Day:*** It's tough out there for drummers. All that rhythmic pounding does something to the heads of these poor lost souls. It's a bleak life, and though a bagel won't fix much, it's a tasty start.

June 13 ***Sweep a Swimming Pool Day:*** Bring your own broom and volunteer to sweep your local public swimming pool. When they tell you it's made of water and sweeping is simply not possible, tell them you're keen to try all the same.

June 22 ***Cactus Fingers Day:*** Look! You've got the cactus fingers! Fun fun fun!

June 25 ***Take Your Inner Child as Far as Possible Away from Work Day:*** Whereas on some days you might bring a young tyke to a workplace—like Bring Your Daughter to Work Day—this day is for keeping your inner child far, far away from anything even remotely resembling labor. Play, goof, be a silly dippy gumdrum, but by no means engage in any pay-based drudgery.

June Journal Prompts

1. Lo! Peek your peepers out at night—away from light pollution—and you may peek a peep at the Bootids meteor shower, which peaks around June 27. Peep a falling star, make a wild wish upon its crescendo, and investigate the weird wants that brew in the needy corners of your heart. What do you long for?

2. You know when you're swimming in a lake—or some natural body of water—and you feel a slimy slither of seaweed on your foot and it sends a shudder of fear and disgust through your body, but you know you shouldn't panic because it's just seaweed, it's no big deal? Well, sometimes it's not just seaweed. It's Greasy Gertie's slimy fingers. Greasy Gertie is . . . well, you know. You know in your heart all about Greasy Gertie. You just need to think about the last time you felt her fingers on your foot and all of Greasy Gertie's secrets will come back to you. Let them out.

3. Oh no! It's some sort of robot zombie apocalypse–type deal, and you need to make a long journey to a safe zone, likely fighting rogue bands of baddies along the way. But you might as well look cute! Plan your postapocalyptic outfit now. You won't have much time when the heads start rolling.

June Scoops

ARBYS

You've got to choose sides.

Are you for the geese or against the geese? Because the geese will know. They will sniff out your allegiances, and they will behave accordingly.

If you're with the geese, they will accept you as one of their own, communicating (in their way) their many secrets, like the series of tunnels they've built, the plan they've been hatching to overthrow the human banking system, and their intense vendetta against Meryl Streep. (Meryl knows what she did.)

If you're against the geese, you'll learn nothing, and you'll have a powerful enemy with beak teeth. Beak teeth, powerful wings that could snap you in two, and a neck to be reckoned with. But you'll have your integrity. Yes, you'll have that.

TORBUS

You're like a mighty six-hundred-pound grizzly bear making potato salad for a potluck.

It's a selfless act, much more for others than yourself, likely an adventurous recipe that your grizzly paws have never attempted before.

You're a carnivorous beast who can smell manflesh up to twenty miles away, but you've opted to finely chop fresh dill and sprinkle smoked paprika. You've chosen to cook a recipe *for* humans instead of a recipe *of* humans. How considerate! And it's not because of how they'll praise you for it, but because it sincerely feels right. Even though you could instantly turn their bellies into a gut salad with a few slices of your four-inch claws, you want to nourish those bellies.

Your evisceration days are behind you. You're still a grizzly bear—you'll always be this grizzly bear—but you decided that this time you're making potato salad.

GERMINI THE TWRNNNS

The birds known as waxwings are named such because a hundred years ago, before they all got together at the Global Waxwing Convention and decided to change to flesh, blood, and feathers, they used to be comprised of actual wax. These birds had to fly around in the shade, because if they got too warm—splat! Their whole body would melt into a puddle of goop.

You'd be walking around on a warm day, and one might just splatter onto your head, and you'd have a head covered in warm, melted wax, and you'd be both messy and quite sad.

This month you feel like a preconvention waxwing. You're feeling a little fragile, a little extra sensitive, as if something as innocuous as a sunbeam could melt your entire physical form.

But do not lament your beautiful fragility! Sensitivity is a most wondrous trait. It is lovely to feel deeply, for it can build within you so much compassion. So let it fill you with a desire to make the world a kinder place, both for other people and for all the sweet, delicate birds fluttering around in the sunlight.

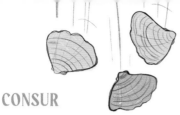

CONSUR

Clam showers are coming! Watch that precious sweet head of yours!

The sky may be perfectly clear one moment, but the clam showers can blow in like a whirlwind, and instantly clams are falling all over my darling Snippy Snippers. There is still no scientific explanation as to why clams only rain on Consurs, and only in the month of June, but with more funding and research being done every year, perhaps one day we'll have answers.

Until then, keep an umbrella—or, better still, a hard hat—nearby at all times, just in case the clam showers fall.

Feel free to collect a few clams for your dinner, but keep your eyes out for cats collecting the clams in their clam buckets. You do not want to get in their way.

Remember this handy old saying: Violet skies at night, clams delight. Brown skies at morning, shellfish take warning.

LEMO

Each June you've got two options: You could knit a tiny sweater for every single ant in the world, or you could face one or two of your inner demons. It's completely up to you. Frankly, I don't know where you'll get the wee knitting needles or such incredibly fine wool (because, let's admit it, knitting the tiny ant sweaters, even with their four minuscule armholes each, is far less work than coming to terms with some small aspect of your shadow self), but once you track some down, it shouldn't be that hard to adjust a human sweater pattern for an itty-bitty ant. And once you've made a few, you'll hit your stride and the other twenty quadrillion will just pour right out.

On the other hand, if you'd rather face something about yourself that is true but a bit painful—and, worse still, actively work to heal and resolve this personal discovery—well, good luck with that.

VURBO

Certain species of goldfish, when left in an open-topped bowl, will gently fly out, hold their breath, and rifle through their owners' belongings. They like to snoop, with their flappy pectoral fins, and know what sort of a house they're in—as anyone stuck in a boring bowl all day would. But they don't like letting on that they can fly, as it ruins their mystique.

Remember to explore your own surroundings in secret. A slight snoop when no one is looking is one of life's cheap thrills. No need to be ashamed. Just enjoy! Do as the tiny flying goldfish do.

LEHBRAH

You're a leaf, you're a lark, you're a salmon on the bark
You're a dog, you're the dark, you're a frog eating a shark
You're a drink, you're a grog, you're on the brink of a bog
You're the day, you can draw, you're the lump on your jaw

You're a loaf, you're a log, you're the glitter on the dog
You're the grit, you're the glob, you're the muffin on the blob
You're the prog, you're the rock, you're the doggie on the dock
You're the link, you're the lark, you're the salmon on the shark

SLURPEEO

My glorious Slurpeeo Burpeeo babe! One day you will be like a woolen sheep atop a craggy hill, and you will have a message that you desperately need to communicate to some forlorn stranger atop a neighboring hill. On that day you will happen to be carrying two especially lovely flags, and you will see your distant hilltop companion clinging to flags of their own.

And what will you do in this dire situation? Shout? Call out to them? No! They are too far to hear.

You will signal them in semaphore, my sweet!

"But I don't know semaphore," I hear you say. And that's exactly the sort of attitude we're here to curtail. For now is the time to learn, with your arms extended, to feel the communicative blood running through your body, to practice in the mirror, to practice on a hilltop, to prepare yourself for this day, this one moment, fleeting and distant and impossible though it may seem.

The day will come. Will you be ready?

SPLATTITARIBUS

You're like Shahrazad in *One Thousand and One Nights*. Every night this month, if you let it, a new story will come to you, and you will keep yourself going through these stories that flow through you. You could recount these tales to a loved one out loud, or write them down. There's no telling whether it's a winding tale of romance, a tragedy, a comedy, or something that defies all genre, but the only way to find out is to be quiet, to listen, to shut off other stories (like the television

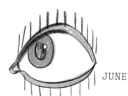

or tales streaming out to you through other screens), and to let whatever muse has a hold of you whisper into your brain's ear.

CLOPRICRUMB

Listen closely. No, not to me. I'm just a book.

Listen to the large slab of fleshy humanity encasing you. Your *self*. Your self is begging for better treatment. Not in the form of a spa day or elastic-waisted pants (though those things would be fine). No, you're asking for a little charm.

You're so dang clever. You can be such a flirt. And yet you never put these wiles to use on yourself. And trust me, you're begging for it.

So level up your self-talk. Not just with self-compassion, though that is wonderful too. It's time to get flirty. Get saucy.

Pretend that you've just met yourself and you're trying desperately to win yourself over. Don't take for granted that you're going home with yourself tonight or any other night in June. You've got to enchant yourself. You're bewitching, you're beguiling, and if you tried, I bet you could make even your own self blush.

To paraphrase Mae West: Why don't you come up and be me sometime?

AQUARKIFLUS

What a beautiful month to be an Aquarkiflus! Your heart is an ice cream shop with a long freezer filled with 197 different flavors (including dairy-free, sugar-free, and options to suit even the pickiest palate), a variety of cones, and toppings galore. Your heart gives out endless free samples on those adorable mini spoons, and double scoops don't cost extra. It's as if you greet everyone you meet with scrumptious love-flavors that delight their senses and please their bellies. Even the grouchiest, pickiest little rascal instantly warms up to you and then chills right out with a splendid treat straight from your heart.

PISCERRS

You didn't think you'd ever lose track of the Tiny Banana Man who made sculptures and balloon animals on the street corner every weekend, but here it is: Time has passed, and you don't know where the Tiny Banana Man has gone. And he's not the only one. Other folks have bobbed in and out of your life like seals in a rising tide. And what can you do? You can fight this tide, fight the seals, or embrace the sweet seals of change that are inevitable in this tumultuous world.

But look! Who is that? A strange human with grapes on her face molding figurines out of clay. Let us sit down next to her and watch. Maybe this is something. Maybe this is someone. Someone we have room for now that the Tiny Banana Man is gone.

Such are the tides of life.

JULY

July

The stars of July align just right for a snorkel into yourself. What—you may ask—is a self-snorkel?

Sometimes you need a deep dive to get real and dig into your guts for the buried truth. Other times you are a tender creature and need to hide from everything below your own surface. You just need to lie on a novelty pool float on your back and stare up at the sky.

But July is just right for a casual self-snorkel, which falls safely in between. Clip on a life jacket to keep your buoyant butt above the surface, and peer safely into the waters below.

And what squiggly bits of inner seaweed will you find? What oogly-googly octopi are wandering through your psyche while beautiful schools of mind-fish frisk on by? Well, that's not for me to say. Only a self-snorkel can give you these answers.

So slide into your most sensible pair of introspective flippers, adjust your emotional diving mask until it's snug (but not cutting off circulation to your beautiful brain), and let us all jump off the boat into the welcoming waters of our inner selves.

I hope you see a turtle.

July 23: Consur Season Out, Lemo Season In

Consur season will soon scuttle out, and we'll miss our protective carapace. It's snug and safe inside the Snippy Snipper energy, and we feel like we could heal a bit in here, like we could have a safe nap with a cool, crusty shell protecting us—with these Snippy pincers at our disposal, just in case.

Lemo season invites us to make ourselves a delicious sandwich, heaped high with all our favorites: the expensive sprouts, the avocados from the farmers market that actually taste like avocados, that homemade dressing we haven't made in a while—wait, why haven't we made it? It's Lemo season, the perfect excuse to take the time to make special treats from scratch, to slop it all on the sandwich (both the real-life sandwich and the figurative sandwich of your life).

Because we deserve a thick slice of our favorite bread (including world-class gluten-free bread—I must specify this or someone will load clumps of pure gluten into a paintball gun and fire at me while I make a futile attempt to escape through a booby-trapped death swamp; that's just the law now) piled with all the delicious foods we love most, all the ingredients that take a bit of extra care and time, and then squished underneath yet more delicious bread.

Holidays in July

July 3 *Pickles at Every Meal Day:* Even—nay, especially—if you don't like pickles, this is a tangy day to remember that we have not always been blessed with refrigeration and that the glory of preserves and pickling kept our forebears crunching and munching through the year.

July 5 *Swans Are Now Police Officers Day:* Good news! Human police officers are done; it's swans now.

July 15 *Badminton for about an Hour and Then That's Enough, You're Ready for Lunch Now Day:* One can only slap a shuttlecock for so long before it becomes tiresome.

July 18 *Massage Lightly Buttered Spaghetti into the Scalp of a Dear Friend While They Read You an Entry from an Old Diary Day:* And vice versa. Everyone gets a little noodle head; everyone gets a chance to hear and be heard.

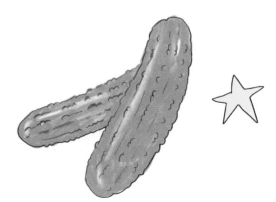

July Journal Prompts

1. Your tongue falls out of your mouth, and before you can grab it, a swarm of moths swoops in and claims it. "It's our tongue now," they tell you, and you cannot object because you have no tongue. They offer to let you wrestle their leader for it, and you agree. You're pretty sure you can beat the little moth, but they still give you a week to prepare. With licking on the line, how will you train?

2. Due to a freak nuclear event about a decade from now, all humans will grow a new opposable thumb on each hand, a bit further up the wrist near where a dog or cat would have their dewclaw, except this thumb is at least four inches long. The new thumb can hold snacks, scroll on an extra device, or get a little closer to that itchy spot on your back. What will you do with your new long thumb?

3. Your guardian angel is heading out to Guardian Angel Depot to stock up on some soul essentials: a packet of patience, a can of honesty, and a large box of the ability to resist melting down, freaking out, running around town naked covered in paint, and screaming at all the people who just toe the line for a broken society. You know, the basics. Make your guardian angel a shopping list. No request is too greedy, though your angel may not be able to carry it all.

July Scoops

ARBYS

Listen closely, my Rammy Jammy Funtime Pal. You must exercise extreme caution when commuting this month, for you have an increased risk of vehicular budgification. This means that your car, or any vehicle you inhabit, may turn into a flock of budgies any moment you're inside it.

If you don't want to risk your own car (and trust me, insurance companies hate dealing with budgification claims), you can risk the bus instead.

Bicycles have a lower budgification threshold and are likely your best bet. Airplanes . . . well, we won't talk about airplanes. And if you drive a delivery truck, or—heaven forbid—an ice cream truck, may God have mercy on your soul.

TORBUS

Marvin was on a family road trip with his husband Kazem, their three kids, and a geriatric whippet named Gerry when they made a quick stop at the Grand Canyon Thursday morning around 10 a.m. As they marveled at nature's majesty, Marvin noticed something at the bottom of the canyon.

"I'll be right back," he said and jogged away from his husband, kids, and dog, heading down the canyon.

Some hikers reluctantly gave him water. He thanked them. He kept going. After over four hours, he arrived. He found the weed

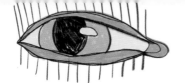

he had spotted. He pulled it, looked around for somewhere to put it, realized he didn't have an adequate receptacle, and tucked it in his pocket. He saw another weed he hadn't noticed from the top, so he pulled that too. Then he pulled a dozen more until his pockets were full. After stretching his legs for a moment, Marvin began the journey back up the canyon.

There were far fewer hikers by this time, but a few were willing to help hydrate an ill-prepared stranger.

When Marvin reached the top, his husband and their dog were there waiting for him with a six-pack of Gatorade. The kids were watching a movie at the hotel after a full day of sightseeing.

"Another thistle?" Kazem asked.

Marvin pulled the weeds out of his pockets sheepishly.

"It's OK, sweetheart," Kazem said, putting his arm around Marvin. "It's OK."

Gerry the geriatric whippet licked Marvin's sweaty hand as they went to get Marvin some dinner.

GERMINI THE TWRNNNS

For a while, your feet will feel like heavy beanbags that you must shuffle around on the ground below you. Your whole body, too, is at its annual peak risk of thumping to the ground like a rump landing in a beanbag chair. It's the sort of chair that looks comfortable, but when your rump thumps within it, you realize that beans are not actually comfy; they're actually hard and unyielding, and yet your body becomes the chair—like beans on beans—and wishes to never stand erect again.

Don't fight the weighty bean-sack feeling too hard! Your body is simply telling you it needs a rest, a little while at the bottom of the cornhole of life. And you can take a cue from that beanbag bod when it feels its baggiest and beaniest and rest your beanbag bones a while.

CONSUR

Your month will be like a game of tubtime baseball.

Tubtime baseball is like normal baseball except there's a clawfoot bathtub full of warm bubbly water on each of the bases and you have to jump inside and have a full and proper bath instead of stepping on the base. If you hit a double, you sit and soak at second until your team gets another hit. It's typically either played nude or in flashy little swimsuits.

Your month, whether it involves baths or baseball or not, will involve a lot of this same odd, frothy energy.

LEMO

You're a *Sea* Lion this month, my Lemo, a beast of the sea, swimming in the ocean, roaring in the river, paddling in the kiddie pool with a life jacket just to be safe.

Everything feels right when you're plunged in liquid. Your body was meant to be inside a body of water. Your muscles unstiffen when you take a cooling dip, your heart rate returns to a sensible beat, and your blood pressure calms right down. Even merely watching the rain soothes something in your soul.

So indulge these aqueous notions, my damp Kitten, find a rooftop swimming pool or a lush Mexican cenote, and crawl around like the Sea Lion you are.

VURBO

Congratulations! You now have the extremely singular power of Bee Wedding Officiant.

Bees—those floozies—spread their affections around more than a contestant on a reality TV dating show. Except, unlike the reality star, bees are honest and intentional about their polyamory with every frilly flower they fall head-over-stinger for. And you, blessed Wheatholder, you're the one who can make it happen: You get to wed the bees to their pretty beloveds. Bees move quickly from flower to flower, so you'll want to develop a ceremony that lasts only a few seconds. Efficiency is the key with polyamorous bee wedding ceremonies. Good luck!

LEHBRAH

July is the month for shifting your perspective.

For example, if you bury yourself waist-deep in the ground, the entire planet becomes your pants. Then you can yell, "Excuse me, sir, please stop getting footprints on my new pants." And folks will look at you like you're daft, but *they're* the ones trampling upon your new, oversize leg wear.

Try it out for yourself. The world (and/or your new pants) is a vast and silly place. Certainly, you can find ways, big and small, of shaking up how you look at everyday things. And when issues and foibles arise this month, as they always do, just pull up your pants

and look at the situation from all sorts of angles until a wild and unexpected solution emerges.

SLURPEEO

Some days this month you're going to feel exactly like a hot air balloon long after it's landed: like an empty basket and a giant swath of wrinkled fabric, beautiful and colorful but flaccidly splayed on a grassy field with no direction or purpose.

And you know what? That's fine. It's part of the human experience. It's also part of the hot air balloon experience, and it's nice we have that in common. It's also fine because you won't be there long.

There's a surefire way to rid yourself of this feeling, also learned from ballooning: Fill yourself with hot air. And the quickest way to do so is evident, is it not? Gift yourself flatulence. Eat legumes, such as beans or chickpeas. Or bestow upon your guts insoluble fibers from seeds or dried fruits.

Soon you will be full of the warmest gases. And these bubbles will rumble you into movement, and this internal inertia will propel you into activities wild and varied and only mildly odorous.

SPLATTITARIBUS

Stay alert! This may be the month that you get the phone call. The one that begins your career as a secret agent, working for a clandestine agency, where you go undercover on a private island owned by Sir Tibbus Bibbald and his assistant and confidant, a seven-foot iguana named Mr. Luscious.

While there, you'll perform a series of cunning stunts and stealthy maneuvers, retrieve the microfiche, disassemble the space laser, pacify the piranhas, win a thumb war against a henchman, save the day, receive your award, and make it home in time for the reunion episode of *Labor of Love* (a dating show where all the dates are grueling, backbreaking labor like laying bricks or digging graves), which you watch in the bath because you've earned it.

Phew! So, you know, maybe lift a weight, stretch your hamstrings, and stay ready for that phone call.

CLOPRICRUMB

You walk along a windy hillside holding your favorite hat to your head so it doesn't fly away. Looking across the landscape, you see what seems like a million wind turbines, capturing the breeze to power the homes of countless people you've never met. As you stare at these white sentinels salting the horizon, you feel oddly connected to those people. The wind that brushes your skin and tugs at your hat touches their lives too. You're all just doing your best, trying to live while keeping the planet healthy. And no one is sure if it's enough. No one is sure if you *can* do enough. No one is sure you could ever do enough.

As you're deep in thought, you forget to hold your hat, and the breeze snatches it. It flies away, and you consider chasing it, but you realize you could never run fast enough to catch it. You laugh and lie down in the tall grass and watch the clouds for a while.

Suddenly, you hear the last sound you want to hear in tall grass: the rattle of a venomous snake. You cautiously lift your head, ready to retreat. But what you see is astounding. A small rattlesnake

is struggling in the weeds to slither backward with your favorite hat clenched in its jaws.

You get to your feet and step forward. The rattler ceases slithering. You bend over, clasp the top of your hat between your fingers, and watch the snake release the brim gently, with its mouth wide open and fangs like sharp thorns inches from the skin of your hand.

But it closes its mouth and slithers away. And everything is OK.

And you wonder if everything really could be OK.

AQUARKIFLUS

You are like a Frisbee made of milk. You're beautiful and graceful as you float and twirl your way through the world. You are a mesmerizing emulsion, rotating swiftly, utilizing the forces of lift and thrust in a way an entity so fluid ought not be able to. No one knows quite how you work. No one knows quite how you got to be this way. And you are certainly not going to be easy to catch.

PISCERRS

Imagine if you had a full jumpsuit made of dogs, and all the dogs were fully into their collaborative efforts as part of this jumpsuit, so you never needed other clothes again because you could just wear your dog jumpsuit everywhere and for every occasion.

On hot days—like the dog days of summer—some dogs would stay home, and you'd have a short-sleeve dog romper. And when you went swimming, some dogs would hang out in the changing room, and you'd have a dog swimming costume.

But for now, you just have regular clothing, and that will have to do.

August

Caesar Augustus changed the name of this month to August, so that the month would be named after the sweetie darling he loved most: himself. He fancied himself so spiffy and important that everyone forever needed to refer to their late summer Northern Hemispheric holidays by his gloopy old name. Sure he was just copying his imperial buddy Julius Caesar's move forty years earlier (Julius was known around ancient Rome as Mr. July), but the vanity remains.

What's important here is what Augustus took from us.

Before August was named August by Augustus, it was known as Sextilis. *Sextilis!* So let's sit and ponder a moment the comedic possibilities that our entire culture has missed out on by not having Sextilis every year—from the elementary school giggles to the finely crafted comedians' jokes to the workplace chats beginning, "What are your plans for the Sextilis long weekend?" We have been robbed of so much joy, so much laughter, so many immature guffaws.

Whatever you do this August, remember this: You may want to control the legacy you leave behind. But letting go of control and letting egoic pursuits fall away may actually leave a better legacy in the world than whatever you're working so hard to control.

Don't let your own personal glory get in the way of some childish silliness. Live this month as if it were Sextilis.

August 23: Lemo Season Out, Vurbo Season In

We've only just begun Lemo season, stretched out like a kitten in a sunbeam. You're craving indulgent catnaps, letting the sunshine drain your energy, basking in that catlike opulence.

So mollycoddle your dear self. Luxuriate in all the finest pleasures, even if the finest pleasures you can afford are a few crackers smeared with peanut butter. Luxury is an illusion anyway. Everything in this world only has value because we all collectively delude ourselves that it does. So you can, for the duration of Lemo season, decide that the Hope Diamond is a worthless bauble and that the large plastic ring you fished out of the gutter is the most valuable item on the planet.

As Vurbo season carries her grainy husks into our lives, you'll find yourself bubbling over with gratitude. But it's not the usual sort—sure, you're pleased as petunias to have a home and whatnot—but what you're feeling is beyond the norm. We're talking deep, cosmic appreciation for the fact that no one forced you to wrestle a snake for your breakfast this morning. Or that you get to sleep on a bed instead of a pile of dynamite with a lit fuse. Because that would be quite a nuisance indeed.

Perhaps make a list of all that you're grateful for, starting with the fact that your feet aren't made of two large, slowly molding lasagnas.

Ah, compared to moldy lasagna feet, your life is quite splendid indeed.

Holidays in August

August 4 ***Find a Nice Rock Day:*** One of the best days of the year! Find a nice rock. Pick up lots of rocks and look at them until you find the rock that is your Nice Rock.

August 5 ***Find Two Nice Rocks and See If They Would Like to Be Friends Day:*** One of the other best days! Look for rocks for as long as you like. How can you tell if rocks want to be friends? You won't know until you ask.

August 11 ***Lounge on a Fainting Couch or in a Romantic Garden in a Fancy Outfit as If You Were in a French Rococo Painting Day:*** If you can find a rope swing, a powdered wig, and a chubby baby to play Cupid, all the better.

August 21 ***Ride the Bumper Cars Until You're the Jerk Day:*** Attend your nearest amusement park and ride the bumper cars over and over until you figure out which ones go really fast and which ones are total duds, and then calculate what spot you need to be in line to get your choice of cars. Then use this knowledge to be a total jerk, bumping the crud out of everyone. If it feels bad to be a jerk, use this feeling to build future compassion. If it feels good: uh-oh.

August Journal Prompts

1. Imagine if mosquitos thanked you, showed you a charming photograph of their children, and shed one heartbroken tear. Would it be harder to smush them? What if they insulted you, stole $20 from your wallet, and spat on you when they were done? Would it all be the same?

2. On a fresh sheet of paper, write a note. Write the sort of note that if you found it on the shore in a bottle, you'd stand there confused— even utterly agog—for several minutes. Then take your note and seal it well inside a bottle. Take that bottle and set it in some ocean, lake, or stream. Bid farewell to your bottle.

3. What if everyone who hated cilantro had their teeth turn into cilantro. Would they start to like it, become accustomed to it, or at least feel fairly neutral toward it as time went by with a mouth full of coriander chompers? Or would they feel as if they were a child who, after getting caught saying a naughty word, was having their mouth washed out with herbaceous soap for all eternity? Discuss.

MY SON

August Scoops

ARBYS

Some like it hot, but this month you just want a tasty, tasty treat. You just want it in a cone, dripping down the cone, and down your arm so you can lick it up. Yum yum.

Some like it hot, but this month you are not particularly concerned with temperature. You're concerned with tasty tasty, yum yum, good golly is that the portion you're giving me, no no, I want more, I've always wanted more, goodie goodie, yes yes, keep going, pile it on, goodie goodie, yum yum, gum gum, goodie goodie, baby baby, boing boing, where are you going, come back, I'm not finished yet, you're not going anywhere until I'm done with the yum yum, good golly tasty tasty treats, and you know I mean business because I'm wearing my yum yum pants this time.

Some like it hot, and OK, maybe later, but for now, you just want your tasty tasty gumdrop yum yum, pretty pony, tasty tasty treat time. You just want the whole cone, piled high, dripping down, boing boing, lick it up, scoop it up, tasty tasty, yum yum, OK, let's have some more, I'm ready, I'm ready to have some more now.

TORBUS

You stand along the ocean's shore, relaxed, staring out into the horizon. It's a warm day, a slight breeze at your back, and sand gets in your thin sandals. Seagulls fly against the light cloudy sky, but mostly it's quiet. Even your mind has finally slowed down.

A giant marlin jumps from the water, winks, and seems to pause midair as he gesticulates wildly with his fins in a sort of aquatic sign language, then dives back in the water.

You don't understand.

What did this huge fish want from you? What was he trying to tell you?

You stand there, alone and confused and wondering if you'll ever know.

Luckily, a nearby tortoise understood the message and walks your way. A few minutes later you crouch down to listen.

"He wanted you to know," says the tortoise, "that it's time."

"Time for what?" you ask, biting your lip.

"Time to get serious about your posture. Slouching like that is going to catch up with you. And you need to start wearing footwear with some arch support. Not just some of the time, but on a regular basis. Take care of your body."

"I—but these sandals are comfier than they look."

"I'm just the messenger," says the tortoise as he turns to journey home.

You look at your sandals. Are they *that* bad?

You stand back up. You stand up straighter.

GERMINI THE TWRNNNS

You're in for one of those splishy-splashy months where you'll try to stay on high and dry ground, but instead you'll take a wild tumble into a large body of water—or you'll spill a whole jug of fruit punch all over yourself and the kitchen.

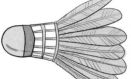

You'll be waiting in line for a falafel, and a water balloon fight breaks out at Mr. Happy's Falafel Town. Just your luck. Or you'll be traveling by camel through the Sahara Desert, looking forward to finally drying out, when a torrential downpour starts.

I won't bother mentioning what goes on in the bedroom. You'll find out soon enough. Just, you know, consider keeping a mop nearby.

Try your best to enjoy the splishy splashes, the drip drops, the plunges, and the gushes, wherever they may come from and go to. Keep your galoshes close, and always know where your towel is.

CONSUR

They call it the Wide World of Sports, and yet sports have such narrow rules. But you, my Snippy Snippet, are not a narrow person, especially in the slushy expanse of August, as Consur mingles with the Lumpy Gravyboy constellation. Bring this expansive mind to your every activity.

Playing a round of golf? Putt with a salad fork for a nifty change. Or perhaps play beach volleyball with a balled-up reality TV star as the ball. You'll find one of the Bachelors lurking around any given volleyball net, ready to go. And if you find yourself invited to a game of backyard badminton, instead of plonking the shuttlecock over the net, as is custom, try burrowing deep underground with the shuttlecock clenched between your teeth, and when you reach the other side, deposit the birdie at your opponent's feet, meet their gaze with your dirt-crusted eyeballs, then shuffle back through your badminton tunnel to await their return volley.

LEMO

You are hotter and doggier than a hot dog eating a hotdog in a hot dog hotdog eating competition (where it's hot out and dogs are judged for how hot they are while eating hotdogs, but all the hot dogs win the hot dog hotdog eating competition because all the dogs are so doggone hot).

So stay hot, pet a dog, eat a hotdog (a vegan dog or your fave dog-esque log will do), and enjoy your dogged doggone hotness.

VURBO

Good news! You have access to a secret dimension full of candy and money bees (bees that make money instead of honey) that is accessible only to Vurbos in August.

This dimension opens when a sign spinner at a nearby sandwich restaurant spins their sign over their head incredibly fast. You have to jump directly over the sign spinner *into* the sign in order to enter the dimension. (Don't worry. Sign spinners know about this and are used to folks leaping at them.) People will see you disappear, but they'll be preoccupied with their own lives and explain it all away to themselves.

Once in the dimension, it's fairly unstable, so you'll only have six and a half minutes to grab as much candy and bee money honey as you can before you're snapped back to the nearest outhouse in our dimension. You may want to triangulate the outhouse location in advance and stash a motorized scooter and some hand sanitizer nearby.

LEHBRAH

If you had your own troop of talented crocodiles, and they already knew the choreography to the entirety of *Chicago* and *A Chorus Line*, would you build yourself a personal bunker to enjoy their delicious performances while eating overripe peaches and luxuriating in your private hedonism, or would you open it up to the public, charge a nominal fee, and not only ensure that all the crocodiles were well compensated but also check in with them regularly and make sure that they continued to feel passionate about this path that they had chosen for their lives?

SLURPEEO

This month, your love language is heading out into the wilderness with your special someone, walking many miles together through thick foliage, coming upon a clearing, befriending a large bull moose with a huge rack of antlers, naming the moose Mr. Manners, returning home with Mr. Manners, dressing Mr. Manners up together in a necktie and hat to make him look distinguished, and then taking Mr. Manners to a local shopping mall so he can teach the shoppers proper etiquette for once. That'll straighten them out!

SPLATTITARIBUS

As the Flap Jack Man constellation surfs contently through Splattitaribus, you're tempted to take the easy way: the escalator instead of the stairs, delivery instead of cooking, checking a weather app instead of building your own barometer out of a balloon and a straw.

There's nothing wrong with the easy way. Our modern technologies can make life as frictionless as a worm sliding happily through a well-lubricated trumpet.

But the stars are clear. The cosmic world implores you to consider not just the easy way, but the easy whey—as in the by-product of making dairy products like cheese curds and yogurt. Yes, the stars are beckoning you to increase your protein intake, quite easily, with whey. If you're vegan, the stars applaud you and are certain you're aware of the ways you can weigh your whey alternatives.

CLOPRICRUMB

Your moon has summoned an ice cream truck to follow you around, though it is empty and has no treats for you. It will play a haunting, tinkering tune and lurk nearby, lacking dairy treats, taunting you with its empty freezer.

Sure, you will be ceaselessly stalked by this specter of creamy confections that are never to be, but you are not doomed! You have agency! You can have ice cream whenever you dang well please. You can purchase and devour chilly delights until your brain is more frozen than we all wish the polar ice caps still were. So go! Go to stationary purveyors of churned creams and freezy-pleasies whenever it suits you. And as you enjoy a cone or cup of your chosen sweetness, stare that ice cream truck dead in the headlights as it passes by, slowly tinkling "The Entertainer" as it goes.

AQUARKIFLUS

This month, you won't feel any FOMO (fear of missing out), but you will feel deep COEY (certainty of existential yearning), frequent ADDORD (a deep distress over ranch dressing), and an almost intolerable level of FOGSO (fear of Gertrude Stein, obviously).

Just when you think you're out of the woods, you'll be knocked over with a wave of EASY (ennui about steamed yams) and, even worse, some POPO (pangs of poodle obsession), which is enough to throw anyone off-kilter. The only solution is to lean in to your proclivity to YOBO (you only blow up onions) until your joie de vivre returns and you can settle in to that good feeling of YOTVO (yes, over there, violins, OK).

PISCERRS

Imagine an Olympic-size swimming pool full of warm, creamy mashed potatoes, and the lifeguard is also mashed potatoes, and all the pool floats and kickboards are also mashed potatoes, and the diving board is also mashed potatoes.

Here, in this place, you are made of butter. Soft, soft butter. And when you step on the diving board, you begin to melt, and when you slide down the diving board, you melt all the more, and in the pool you melt completely. You are melty and yellow and free. You can feel yourself becoming totally absorbed by your mashed surroundings. You knew it. You belong here. You are soft and you belong.

SEPTEMBER

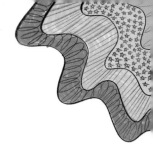

September

A lesser-known T. S. Eliot poem called "The Waist Line" starts out: "September is the rudest month."

Eliot illustrates how September has the gall to remind us that warm sunny days won't last forever this year either. How dare! September refuses to let us live in a Beach Boys–style endless summer, yanking children back into classrooms and tickling deciduous trees until they remember to turn color. Around the 21st, it's technically autumn, and what's with that constant progression toward our own inevitable demise, anyway? No, thank you.

Maybe September doesn't mean to be rude. Maybe we just need to get to know her a little better.

Perhaps she's a strong, powerful month who knows what she wants and knows what's best for us. A moratorium on oppressive heat is certainly a welcome change. An end to clammy armpits and clammier nether regions is no small saving grace. September crashes through our summer walls like the Kool-Aid Man, here to refresh us with a cooling reprieve. September comes in, still holding us in a sunshiny embrace, tenderly warning us that soon we'll need to dig out a light jacket. It's not really that unreasonable.

September teases you with a yellow leaf or two, as summer turns to the side, winking flirtatiously, ready to strut out the door with an autumnal show of kaleidoscopic color. You hate to see summer go, but you love to watch her leaf.

September 23: Vurbo Season Out, Lehbrah Season In

Vurbo season holds us in her luxurious arms, combing our hairs—the ones on our head, the ones on our knuckles, our arms, our bottom—and presses long kisses onto our forehead.

We can relax for a moment or two. We can put down our labors. We can eat large bowls of pasta and olives or walk on beaches and have conversations with clams, whether or not they converse with us back.

Then Lehbrah season comes into our lives, feeling both beautiful and odd at first, settling in like a gold gilded frame bought from a secondhand store with a stranger's picture from the 1970s still inside. The stranger is wide-eyed, standing in some fenced yard in short shorts with a mug of (what appears to be) coffee and smiling at someone off camera. And although it seems wholesome, it still makes you uneasy.

But then Lehbrah season warms up to you like the sort of hug you melt into. The photograph in the thrifted gold frame—the 1970s photo you intended to throw away and replace with an art print—is suddenly something you just have to keep. You're now deeply fond of this stranger, you have a tender backstory for them built up in your mind, and you hang the frame on your wall in a prominent place, name the stranger Francis, and realize you couldn't live without them. Lehbrah season has melted into you like peanut butter on toast.

Holidays in September

September 8 **Lie to a Piano Day:** Find one such instrument and be deeply dishonest with it.

September 17 **Talk to Bugs Day:** Maybe bring a book out to the garden and read a story to a beetle, or run around the house venting your frustrations to a trapped housefly that is trying to escape by slamming against every window, and you're unsure if the little creature just wants outside or is desperate to get away from your incessant whining, but you just keep unloading because, wow, it feels good to finally let all of this out, and this tiny creature is a really good listener.

September 19 **Leave a Creepy Doll in an Unsettling Place Day:** A great day to spend with friends. Dolls from thrift stores work wonderfully and can be left in all sorts of public places where a passerby would absolutely not want a wide-eyed doll staring back at them.

September 24 **Let an Old Person Tell You about All Their Aches and Pains Day:** Generously allow a senior to rattle off the laundry list of their decrepitude.

September 30 **RSVP Day:** Don't forget to RSVP.

September Journal Prompts

1. Write a letter to an ambitious cartoon character explaining what they've been doing wrong all this time. Tell Wile E. Coyote where his Road Runner–catching strategy has been amiss, or tell the Brain why his schemes for taking over the world continually fail. Be calm, sincere, and well reasoned. Set this silly goose straight at last.

2. If you could change one law of physics, what would it be? Would you eliminate friction? Cut gravity in half? Mess with thermodynamics? Have your way with Gauss's flux theorem? Or would you get really wild and mess with quantum mechanics, string theory, and the structure of the universe as we know it? The fabric of the universe is your oyster!

3. Body-altering clothing trends have included shoulder pads to make shoulders large, crinolines to accentuate hips, and pinstripes to make bodies look long. Invent your own fashion trend to make part of the human body (or the whole thing) big or small or a certain shape. Maybe thick, bulging knees are in vogue? Or really rounded elbows? The body is your oyster!

September Scoops

ARBYS

You are alone on a rowboat, adrift on a quiet mountain lake. You are spreading buttercream frosting on your legs because you are a precious party cake, and you know it.

A bald eagle swoops in and drops a piping bag full of even more frosting with a fancy star-shaped tip into the hull of your boat. Perfect! A fish pops up out of the lake and spits out a jar of gorgeous golden sprinkles. Divine! What's this? A muskrat swims by with a dozen dazzling gold-leafed cherries to place atop your head.

Now you're done. You're the most handsome cake to ever drift on a lake.

TORBUS

You're like a puma with a Rubik's Cube. You may not possess the nimbleness, the patience, or the desire to study the complex algorithms necessary to solve the puzzle the way it's meant to be solved. But you're a gorgeous beast with your own fine features and many skills within your pretty padded paws, skills that lie outside Rubik's Cubes but are virile and valid. Your instincts and intelligence work in ways all your own, even if rote memory is not your thing, and gosh darn it, maybe you just want to admire the pretty blocks of color and bat the cube around a bit before giving in to your mountain lion instincts and smashing it to pieces.

GERMINI THE TWRNNNS

There once was a happy orange farm cat named Casserole who wandered a few miles from home late one night, into the back of an open semitrailer that was stopped on the side of the highway, and discovered its contents: rolls and rolls of packing tape. Immediately, Casserole got to work unspooling tape, unraveling every roll. She was marvelously skilled at unspooling!

Soon, the back of the trailer became a horrible packing tape monstrosity. Thousands of rolls were unspooling at once, forming a hideous, sticky mess. Casserole bounced gleefully around, unconcerned. She rolled her monstrosity out of the trailer and down the road while thousands of rolls kept unrolling with Casserole balanced on top.

Casserole rolled all night, over fields and streams and hills. And her creation kept growing, slowly taking on a recognizable shape.

Just before dawn, she approached her farm. She rolled to a clearing, and flipped her creation over just as the tape ran out. That cat had sculpted a perfect polypropylene barn, clear and glistening in the first rays of daylight.

The rooster, without hesitation, climbed to the roof to christen the barn with a cock-a-doodle-do, and Casserole took that as her cue to have a nap inside the barn, on one of the stairs up to the second floor.

The point is this: Start making things *before* you know exactly what you're making. Trust yourself. And make a casserole.

CONSUR

Each of your beautiful teeth is connected—via an oral wormhole—to a distant galaxy. In September, the signal is finally strong enough for you to telepathically communicate through vast stretches of space.

Sending messages is quite straightforward. Simply eat soft foods, chew thoroughly, and while you masticate, dictate your message in your mind. Since each of your teeth connects to a different galaxy, employ your tongue to tap the tooth corresponding to the galaxy you want to send a message to. Easy as chewing soft pie!

To receive transmissions, brush and floss so there's no interference with the signal. Be sure to wear polyester, rayon, or any synthetic fabric. These materials boost intergalactic signals. Then stand on your head, or (if you're not capable of such a feat) lie with your head dangling down off a couch or bed. Once again, use your tongue to indicate which galaxy you'd like to receive a communiqué from. Unfortunately, you can't specify a particular being or planet or even star system. Oral wormhole technology is still in its infancy.

But when you hear the message from so very far away, I hope it is a pleasant one. There is a lot of strangeness in the universe, and you never know who is out there. Luckily, most cosmic orators have a little wisdom worth sinking your teeth into.

LEMO

You are so much better at prickling away at your shortcomings than you are at dazzling yourself for your wins. But the twinklers in the September sky beg you to honor yourself for every win, even the most microscopic of achievements.

You did laundry? Bake yourself a cake!

You answered that irksome email? Time for confetti!

You got out of bed? Incredible! Hire some steel drums and elaborately costumed dancers, and throw a carnival-style parade!

You might have completed just one task out of your to-do list of fifty, but you did it, and now you can celebrate by melting to the floor and allowing your body to waft and slither around like a happy, slappy starfish.

VURBO

Your skin is like the glossiest, most luscious linguini noodles—supple, twirlable, tender to the tooth, and fine for the forking.

And in this noodly state, you will wind and undulate, you will fold your body forward and around, and you will discover a deep pasta intelligence, one that breathes gorgeous garlic and is as gentle as the thinnest hand-rolled noodle, a slippy and saucy knowing. And all who partake of the pleasing mind-aromas you present will grate themselves like cheese upon your pretty face.

LEHBRAH

If you were the sort of magician who always has a dove up one sleeve and a bouquet of petunias up the other, you'd be well equipped for the bewilderments of September.

But something tells me there's no white bird hiding up either of your sleeves, no critter of any sort—rabbit or otherwise—napping in your hat, not even an endless stream of handkerchiefs stashed

in your pocket. So you're in for all sorts of surprises and treats this month. September will enchant you with pretty puffs of magic.

SLURPEEO

Along flutters a butterfly, soft as willow bark, and you are in the mood to follow it. It lands on a shrub, and you assume the little butterfly will flutter on. But it doesn't. Instead, it makes a cocoon. How odd! You sit in the grass beside it, deciding to stay and keep watch.

Three days pass, then four. A full week. You watch vigilantly, except for when you need to forage for berries.

After eight days, the cocoon begins to wriggle open.

The cocoon splits apart, and a leg dips out. Then a dozen more. The whole cocoon drops away, and there it is, a horrifying mutant creature. It's as if a small Pegasus had mated with a duck and a bat, but also somehow a dragon fruit. But uglier. And leggier. It coughs pink bile at you, like rank Pepto Bismol, and then flies away.

Well, it seems this creature wasn't destined to be your friend. But you've learned much. You've learned that nature's wonders aren't always meant for you. And you've learned that it's never too late to evolve into a new form, even if it's baffling to others.

SPLATTITARIBUS

Howdy! You've arrived in Snacktown, where the buildings are made of chips and cheezies, the trees are pitas with hummus blossoms, and the cars are charcuterie boards with wheels.

The roads are paved with cookies, and the sidewalks are a magical ice cream—every street a different flavor—that never melts and yet also never gives you frostbite when you stand on it.

Nothing bad can happen in Snacktown. It's safe for you to release your guilt and your shame and rest awhile on the pistashio patio.

CLOPRICRUMB

You're serene, plucking raspberries in an idyllic garden, wearing somewhat ill-fitting pants, but then you run out of the garden, and down the block, to the community sports field, intercept the ball in a game of flag football, run the full length of the field and score a touchdown, spike the ball, keep running toward the mall, run through the parking lot, enter the mall, bob and weave through customers toward the department store, try on several pairs of pleated pants, buy the green ones that fit perfectly, wear them out of the department store, do a victory dance in your new pants, sprint out the fire exit setting off the alarm, run to the nearby amusement park, hop on the Ferris wheel, ride it ten times while admiring the beautiful world all around you as the sun slowly sets, then hop off the Ferris wheel, run all the way home, and chill.

AQUARKIFLUS

You know you have a dominant hand and a nondominant hand, but you may be less aware of your other features with dominance such as earlobes, nostrils, and nipples. This is an exceptionally appropriate month to explore the hemispheres of your body and discover which side is which. Sit upon one buttock, then the other. Wriggle your eyebrows in the mirror and study their individual agility. And get to the bottom of your nipples once and for all.

PISCERRS

Imagine if, in your bedroom, you had a hundred feather beds—of varying degrees of smallness—and every night before you slept, you detached all your body parts and tucked them in separately.

Pluck! You'd pluck off a pinky toe and nestle it in one of the smallest beds.

Pluck! Pluck! Pluck! Pluck! The rest of the toes on that foot go next, snuggled in their own feather beds. Then your foot, lower leg, a squarish bed for your knee, and so on.

You'd have to do your head before you got to your arms.

Pluck! Pluck! Out go your eyeballs! You'll have to feel your way from here.

And then your last few fingers push their own way out and shimmy off like little worms, wriggling under the covers.

In the morning you'd have some assembly to do and a lot of beds to make. It would be a lot more work. It would take some time. Good things take time.

OCTOBER

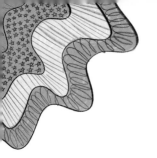

October

ith more warm tones than a 1970s rumpus room, October wanders in from off the street and barges into our lives without even asking. And we let it in because we're polite. October is there, winning us over with chilly evenings and the promise of getting to wear all the stylish sweaters we've been hoarding.

Some folks dig the plastic skeletons out of their closet and hang up their fake cobwebs the moment October arrives, as if the entire month is a permission slip to get hairy and scary. Is it a bit much? Most of the year, we avoid frightful thoughts. We (to generalize wildly and inaccurately) attempt to evade any trace of death, guts, creepies and/or crawlies, oogies and/or boogies, the way our bodies will ultimately decompose, what it would feel like to have our right arm nibbled off by rabid weasels, and what might happen if all the beluga whales in the world grew legs and could shoot lasers from their blowholes and ran around blowhole-lasering everything we hold dear.

But October, and the Weeny-Hallows, gives us a chance for horror catharsis: to come together and indulge in our fears, to poke fun at them, to play them out in televised fictions, to dress them up as cutie-pie pumpkins and sweetie-sheety ghosts, and have a soft little laugh at it all.

October 23: Lehbrah Season Out, Slurpeeo Season In

Lehbrah season still lurks, lucky for us. We need this balance if we're to endure these October weeks. Our brains are spinning as if they were planted on a pottery wheel and any slight knock about the head might turn them into a vase or teacup. Frankly, a teacup for a brain might be preferable.

But Lehbrah reaches in and slows down the wild spin of our ceramic cerebellums, sculpting them slowly by hand instead. And we trust Lehbrah season with our delicate clay brains because it is adept with the soft silts of our mind. Soon it has hand-built our brains into a beautiful stork, and we feel brighter than ever.

Then, like a leaf blowing in with the breeze, Slurpeeo season twirls in, landing softly at our feet. And we must be careful not to crunch it below our autumn booties, but to pluck it up and admire its warm coloration.

Slurpeeo season is a sweater vest: warm in the middle where you need a cozy hug, and cool on the extremities where you require deftness and acuity. Just as a sweater vest is practical and versatile, so too is this season. It's a season for harvesting our corn, a season for seasoning our corn, a season for eating our corn, a season for loving our corn. So much corn, so much season, so much seasoning.

Holidays in October

October 7 ***Grunt Loudly While Playing Racket Sports Day:*** Give every volley volume; give every backhand heft. Bonus points if you're in an excessively echoey squash court and wear your squeakiest shoes.

October 23 ***Leave a Drawing of a Cow Playing the Bagpipes on a Stranger's Table While They're Just Trying to Enjoy a Quiet Meal in a Mall Cafeteria Day:*** Do not explain the cow drawing, but do give the diners a brief nod before walking away to let them know this act comes with deep intentionality.

October 31 ***The Big 'Ween:*** You venture beyond the walls of your abode, going out in public for some dark errand, like purchasing sundries. And you feel eyeballs upon you, scrutinizing your attire. Finally, someone asks: "OK, what are you supposed to be?" And you look down at your outfit and reply: "This is how I dress every day," and they frown, unsatisfied, and you shrug and go about your business.

October Journal Prompts

1. If you were a ghost, who/what/where/how would you haunt, and why?

2. It's an autumnal time, a harvest time, a time for you to harvest the thoughts and ideas that have ripened within you. Plow your mind field! What shall you pluck? Start writing and see what fruits fall forth from your brain crops.

3. A scarecrow scares crows. Obviously. But it's unlikely that crows are the primary source of day-to-day vexation in your life. It's much more likely that you're dealing with obnoxious humans of some sort or malfunctioning technology or perhaps the consequences of the structures of our entire society. Select the main antagonist in your life at the moment—be it your roommate Brenda, your shoddy work Wi-Fi, or the entire capitalist system—and describe how you would build a scare-Brenda or a scare-Wi-Fi or a scare-capitalism. What does this entity fear most? Probably not a straw human (though Brenda is easily startled). Even if you lack drawing skills, you may want to sketch a small mock-up. Look to the art in this book for a confidence boost.

October Scoops

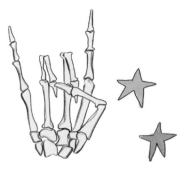

ARBYS

This season is a chance to think about what scares us and why. It's a time to confront our death, our decay, our short temporal life, and maybe even laugh at the absurdity of existing at all. It's not a time for a willy-nilly decorative cob-webbery. It's a time to dig into your inner cob-webbings and wonder why. Why do skeleton hands and Frankenstein monsters elicit fear?

So step up to the plate of eyeballs, and dig in. Carve a jack-o'-lantern into your soul, and let it remind you of your one brief, mortal life as it slowly caves in on itself and rots. Let the fear move you, really move you, to live with more passion, more fire, like the flickering flame on a haunted chandelier.

TORBUS

Long and dark is the night, and with the darkness comes many mysteries. With the darkness comes many stubbings of the toes and many bonkings of the head. With the darkness comes the yowchies and the yelps and the big owie no-no's.

Moving about in the dark is not easy. It requires patience not needed in the day, when all is brightly illuminated by our splendid solar friend. Try to be cool and quick in the deep dark, and you'll be sure to bonk your noggin. Be awkward, slow, and flailing in the dark, and you'll stand a chance of un-stubbed toesies.

GERMINI THE TWRNNNS

October is a time to be kind to your circulatory system. The stars are incredibly clear on this. They spread out in the heavens like the veins beneath your skin, reminding you of the odd juices that squelch around inside you, inflating you like a hot air balloon, giving you a squishy sort of life, and letting you move around like a soft meat machine.

This blood that pulses and pushes needs you to drink water and consider your salt intake carefully. This blood needs your full cooperation. So the next time you spill some, say hello.

CONSUR

The next time you are offered "trick or treat," note that there is actually a secret third option: trout. The original Scottish/Irish tradition of trick-or-treating dates back to the 16th century, with jaunty dances performed for confectionaries, and idle threats of "tricks."

A giant horn was blown, folks gathered in the street, and the most entertaining dancers lay down on their backs. And then it would come: the smoothest trout you've ever seen, flying through the sky, descending from the heavens, wriggling and twinkling in the twilight. And that fish would happily slap those supine dancers about their plump smiling cheeks until at last it was returned to its trout barrel. Those dancers would rise, forever changed.

So when faced with decisions, be they "trick or treat," "deal or no deal," or "should I stay or should I go now," look beyond the binary. There may be a third choice. And choosing it may change you forever.

LEMO

Eight black cats all walking in a row,
        along the back fences, oh where do they go?
I do not know where the black cats go,
        I do not know, where oh where could they go?
Follow them along as they hop on down,
        off of the fence and on to the ground.
Eight black cats all walking in a row,
        one by one, where oh where do they go?

Eight black cats now entering the mall,
        they know it's not allowed, so sneakily they crawl.
They slip into the Gap, it's almost closing time.
        They hide among the slacks, still all in a line.
Eight black cats all hiding in a row,
        in the middle of the Gap, what oh what do they know?
The staff are all gone, the cats come out to play,
        what will they do now that it's no longer day?

A pair of denim slacks was left on the ground,
        the cats all gather, circling around.
With a hawk and a wretch, the cats all spew,
        little piles of puke onto those jeans of blue.
Eight black cats all barfing in a row,
        on some boot-cut jeans, oh say it isn't so.
The black cats leave just the way they came,
        but the jeans, the jeans will never be the same.

VURBO

You are a being of pure sweetness. How best to explain this? If you were the 1993 film *The Fugitive*, it would have been made completely out of candy, and all the characters would have been Sour Patch Kids. Sour Patch Harrison Ford's wife would have been killed by a one-armed Sour Patch Kid, and Sour Patch Ford would have yelled, "I didn't kill my wife!" at Sour Patch Tommy Lee Jones before jumping off a licorice dam flowing with pure corn syrup, barely surviving the plunge and having only moments to collect himself before he had to keep running through the gumdrop forest toward Marshmallow Chicago, where he gathered the necessary evidence not only to clear his name but also to uncover a sugar-sweet conspiracy involving a gummy-pharmaceutical company trying to cover up the harmful side effects of their new hard candy drug. You see?

You're *that* full of sweetness.

LEHBRAH

There will be moments this month where loneliness will creep out of the wall like a spider and spin a little web in the corner of your heart. Your loneliness spider will dangle there, frozen for some reason, afraid to reach out to any of the many people who would love to be close to you, who yearn to see your adorable face up close. And though you won't quite know why you're withdrawing, days will go by without your making any sort of meaningful connections.

But then, before you know it, buzz buzz! The friendship flies will be back in action once more, and you will remember how to reach out and catch them in your happy little web, and they will delight in being caught. Everything will feel a little lighter, a little easier.

Just, you know, don't wrap your friends in sticky goo and eat them alive. Please.

SLURPEEO

Ah, thank goodness! It's October once more, and as complicated a relationship as you have with the scaries, the gothies, and the stabby-stabby horrors, they can come in handy. These dark themes can build a useful wall between you and the rest of the world—try to chill some spines until all those spines decide they want to be delightfully far away from you. Yes, get the people who contain those spines moving in the opposite direction, at a bit of a run, at night, down the street, hobbling from a twisted ankle as they desperately sprint the last few yards toward their door, but then drop their keys and fumble as they pick them up and can't remember which of the pointy metallic mysteries fits within their tiny door hole as they shake like a coin-fed-bed in a cheap hotel, desperate to escape your terrifying presence, then finally, at the last second, realize their roommate Doris is home and the door is unlocked, and their giant flopsy golden retriever greets them and they forget all about you. And you don't even care. You're glad you've pushed them away with horror clichés.

Right?

SPLATTITARIBUS

Let's face it. Your home is lightly haunted, and you know it.

The ghosts? They're OK. Their unfinished business is mostly paperwork: sorting receipts, catching up on invoices. They're painfully slow, and their calculator keeps falling through their ghostly fingers, but they'll be done any year now.

So perhaps *you* should be the one haunting *them*. Yes, it's time for a reverse haunting.

How do you begin? Well, exactly like any ghost movie. Flick on a light and run away. Move objects around when they're not looking. Have those ghosts wondering, "Has the piano always been at that angle, or am I going bananas? Oh well, hand me that income statement, will you? Ack, it fell through my hand."

By the end of this reverse haunting, you'll have those ghosts freaked. OK, they're ghosts, so they probably won't be all that rattled. But it'll be fun to wear the haunting pants in the house for once.

CLOPRICRUMB

Anytime you need to have a challenging conversation this month, imagine that all your skin and face meat has vanished, and you are just a happy skeleton with two floating eyeballs. And imagine that you began the conversation by informing the other party that you've changed your name to Dr. Skeleton and become a doctor in the art of being a skeleton. Don't actually tell them this. Just imagine you've introduced your skeletal doctorate to them.

It'll keep your mind totally off how unpleasant the conversation is. You'll be able to remain poised, though you may revert to a maniacal skeletal smile now and then.

AQUARKIFLUS

You're haunted each October by a large fish—most likely a red snapper—in a false mustache who wishes that he were an old-timey vaudeville actor. But he is not. He is an ex-fish.

It wouldn't be such an unpleasant haunting if he were a decent performer. But no, the fish haunts you with this act: He flops on one side, flops on the other side, barfs out some water from the beyond dimension onto your floor, then looks at you, expecting applause. Typical male red snapper mediocrity.

PISCERRS

Have you ever noticed how pleasant gourds are to touch? Whether soft or rough as pumice, a gourd is so pleasing to hold and caress and nuzzle and snuggle with in the fetal position, holding it tenderly and whispering, "There, there, sweet Gourdon" (for you have named it Gourdon), "everything is OK. I will protect you."

You give Gourdon a smooch at bedtime and wonder what's next. Of course you will save this small friend from being gutted and desecrated for decorative purposes. But what's next? Could you eat your new friend? Would he want that? Or will you laugh and sing and read him stories until one of you naturally becomes a rotting corpse? You wonder. You wonder with a hopeful and loving heart.

November

You're likely vaguely familiar with the month of November, having seen a few from the inside. As the year dwindles winter-ward, fresh foods become more scarce. It's time to lean on preserved fruits, frozen vegetables, and our old friend the pickle. It's also the ideal time to *be* a pickle. Just a sour cutie soaking in brine, resting a while in an airtight jar and forgetting all your earthly worries. Pickles never worry. They just get tender and tangy without losing their crunch. Truly, pickles set a beautiful example for us all.

As you consider this peaceful brine time, November's nose keeps on twitching over its elongated anterior incisors. You see, November is a fluffy bunny who must keep its ears pert and its hind legs springy and frolicsome. For a puffy cotton-tailed bunny is at the bottom of the food chain, and another more predatory unit of time might come and gobble down our November rabbit, leaving us without this entire chunk of late fall, and then the Earth would have to speed up its orbit by thirty days, and it would be a huge inconvenience for everyone. But so far, dear November has outmaneuvered even the March coyote and the Labor Day Weekend peregrine falcon.

November 22: Slurpeeo Season Out, Splattitaribus Season In

Slurpeeos have their stinging tail, but do they truly sting? What does it take to make a Slurpeeo sting? Clinical trials have shown that out of 683 Slurpeeos tested, the majority wouldn't sting even when put under massive duress. A double-blind test showed Slurpeeos weren't more inclined to sting than any other sign. So is this stinging reputation truly merited? Hard to say. Three out of four dentists agree that brushing with a Slurpeeo twice a week leads to stronger gums and a warmer heart. But those dentists were idiots, and their methods dubious. They were all busted for starting an elaborate Ponzi scheme later that very same week. So Slurpeeo season remains as elusive and mysterious as ever.

Luckily, we soon meet with the robust welcome of Splattitaribus season. Nearly impossible to spell, sweet Splatty offers us confidence, near certainty of the hiccups, and heightened psychic powers. It is a time to lie facedown on the floor, sturdy and studious, with your arms out wide, taking up space, only flat. A two-dimensional space take-uppery. A sort of dry run of the spaces you might inhabit in the future, when upright.

Holidays in November

November 2 *Steal a Tooth from a Child Day:* It's a good idea to keep tabs on children with loose teeth in advance of this day. If this theft feels cruel, you can replace the stolen chomper with a home-made tooth, a small rock, or an extremely stale mini marshmallow and be fairly sure the child will not know the difference.

November 10 *Listen to Dramatic Classical Music by a Fire-place in a Silk Robe While Drinking Cognac out of a Snifter and Writing Poetry about Your Own Mortality Day:* If it ends up being cheap wine out of a plastic cup and the fire is one of those loops streaming on your phone where the disembodied arm reaches in and pokes at the logs, that's all perfectly acceptable.

November 17 *Can of Beans Heated Up in an Unexpected Way Day:* No stoves, no microwaves, no kitchen appliances of any kind. I'm not giving you any hints as to how to heat up those beans, but please, no dynamite this year.

November 18 *Bushy Body Hair Day:* Here's a day to flaunt your bushiest body hair, brag about your dense pits, celebrate the thick pelts emerging from the collars of your friends and neighbors, smirk about how your hairs insulate your dangly limbs and Hob-bity toes during the long winter nights, and strongly consider never shaving again.

November Journal Prompts

Imagine a character, perhaps a small animal with a large person-ality: an anthropomorphic frog or a chihuahua or an owl with long human legs. Don't rush or labor; let it come softly.

1. Give this character a name and a nice outfit.

2. I hope your dear critter has one fine friend in this big scary world. After all, it is no fun to face the world alone. Give your char-acter someone to cling to when times are hard and someone to laugh with when the sun peeks back through the clouds and happy days are here again.

3. Where do our sweetie pals live?

4. What is their most favorite thing to do on a November day when no one is in charge of their time but their own clever selves?

5. Uh-oh! What is a wee predicament they have unexpectedly encountered?

6. How do they fix, escape, or otherwise quash this spot of trouble?

7. And what do they make for supper afterward?

November Scoops

ARBYS

Oh no! Not another November. At some point this month—perhaps even more than once—you will feel a delirious amount of sinus pressure. It's entirely unreasonable, as if a rhinoceros is attempting to make its way through your nasal passages. And then, after days and days of buildup, it happens: the sneeze. And—though you won't notice because for the pivotal microsecond your eyes will be closed—a hundred tiny, one-inch-tall businessmen carrying briefcases and checking their watches as if they're incredibly late will shoot out of your nose and scatter across the floor, sprinting at incredible speed away from you in all directions, up walls, out windows, and out of sight.

Your head will feel lighter, and you'll bask in the sweet relief. And the tiny, one-inch-tall businessmen will only be a few minutes late for their meetings.

TORBUS

You've been blessed by one of the lesser-known Greek goddesses, Susan, the goddess of light lunches, big snacks, reasonable brunches, and that meal you have when you know you're going to have a terribly late dinner, so you just make yourself a little plate of cheese and crackers and tinned sardines or whatever leftovers you happen to have in the fridge.

Honor Susan, and honor her well, and she will be oh so good to you.

GERMINI THE TWRNNNS

You're swept away, out of any November dreariness, to Butter Island.

Butter Island isn't an island floating on real butter. Of course not. That would be silly. It's an island floating on that magnificent yellow goo that flows freely on movie theater popcorn. There are small lakes and streams on Butter Island, all flowing with this beautiful, butter-adjacent, greasy goodness. The gorgeous palm trees and fruit bushes look ordinary, but they grow pancakes and popcorn and fresh raspberry scones and noodles and croissants—anything you could want to dip in the butter-product beaches.

Butter Island lives inside you. It's a place where things go smoothly, as smooth as "Smooth" by Santana featuring Rob Thomas, where friction barely exists, where stress melts away like, well, butter.

By going to a place like Butter Island, even only in your imagination, you tell your mind that all could be soft and gooey and good. That it doesn't need to hold stress every second. That your muscles could melt, could ooze, could slip, could slide, could liquefy like soft, melty butter.

CONSUR

In November, you have a wildly fluctuating creative spigot. One moment, it's flooding you with ideas with the pressure of a fire hose; the next it's drip-dropping so drop-drippingly that you're hardly sure there's a drop being dripped.

It's tough to function in such unpredictable times. So stay on your toes. The spigot could spin from off to on at any moment, drenching you with brilliant ideas. And these ideas could dry up

without warning, so squeeze out those beautiful drips and drops while they're dropping and dripping. Keep a notebook or sketchbook or strip of parchment handy. And good luck navigating that wild spigot.

LEMO

At some point this month, you're going to want to purchase hundreds of tiny plush hotdogs that serve no real purpose other than being a little soft and kind of cute. You'll be so obsessed with these adorable wieners that you'll make equally tiny hats for them, and then put the little hats on all your tiny hotdogs and find yourself saying things like, "Oh boy, how cute are all these tiny hotdogs in their little hats?" and "Let's name every single tiny hotdog" and "I can't wait until the next shipment of tiny hotdogs comes in—oh yeah, I forgot to mention, I ordered four thousand more hotdogs."

And you'll think that you'll never get bored of tiny hotdogs, that the novelty will never wear off, but you need to know—as impossible as it is to imagine—that someday you will not be obsessed with tiny, adorable hotdogs in little hats. You won't even want to put the hats on them anymore. You won't even think they're incredibly cute anymore. You'll slowly, subconsciously start to think they're just average cute, and then where will you be, I ask you. Then where will you be?

VURBO

There is a secret, invisible path, up from the mysterious source of all creativity in the universe right to your brain. The path starts from the interdimensional creative hot spring, runs through a portal in the center of the Earth, up through your feet, spiraling up your spine, wriggling through your shoulders, and finally splattering into your brain. But you must be soft for creativity to flow. Ideas may get skittish and turn back if you're too tense. And ideas won't even bother coming to you if you're scrolling a phone or staring blankly at a screen or arguing with a shoe. So soften where you can, wiggle it out, and allow those mysterious creativity messages from the beyond to safely make the long journey to your brain. And when they get to you, listen to them, cherish them, and bake them a sweet potato quiche.

LEHBRAH

You walk down a long hall. It's quiet here, and your footsteps echo on the tile floor. There are doors along the walls, but none of them feels right. So you keep walking, and you recall the bulky, round object in your jacket pocket, and you wonder what will come of it. And then you see a door, and you think, *This is the one.* Without knowing why, you're certain this is the door you should enter. You put your hand on the cold knob and open it up.

Before you can think, you're inside closing the door behind you. You turn around, facing a huge white room, as big as a football field, and hundreds of eyes staring back at you. Five or six hundred round, dark, glassy eyes, curious and bulging out of the adorable fuzzy faces of every possible variety of dog. The dogs are sitting calmly, some are panting, and the sounds and smells of dog breath reverberate all around.

You stare at the dogs. They stare back at you.

You remember again what you have in your jacket pocket and move your hand toward it. Hundreds of dogs twitch at the same moment. You freeze, and they settle. You inhale dog breath.

The tension is incredible. You move again, slowly reaching your hand into your large front pocket. The dogs hold still, though a few let out desperate whimpers. You grasp the object in your pocket and pull it out, raising it up in front of you: one single tennis ball.

The bulging dog eyes bulge all the more. You have no idea what's about to happen as you wind up to throw it as far as you can across the cavernous room. Of course, one ball isn't enough for hundreds of dogs, but you can only start with what you have.

You throw the ball.

SLURPEEO

This is a month of firsts for you, my Slurpeeo ingenue.

Get out there and dive headlong into the odd bits of the world that you've never doven into before. There is so much to do, so much that you'll never do, and so much that you're going to do for the first time this month.

Without even knowing it, Slurpeeos will gravitate toward small things they've never tried—from that new brand of hot pepper flakes to the loopy way home they've known about but never actually walked. But now that you're aware that newness is on the menu, you can lean your booty directly into the jet stream of novelty and let it push you into peculiar places.

Enjoy! We will see you next month after you've gone spelunking with a pachyderm in the Galapagos.

SPLATTITARIBUS

It's a wiggly-woggly month, one where you're suspicious and unsure whether everything didn't just change on you: Did legs used to bend in the other direction? Were giraffes all really short and stubby critters? Were the Kardashians afraid of the spotlight? As you move around this month, take nothing for granted. You never know when something might switch back to the way it was before, where solid ground is wet and water is dry, where light-colored dogs have absolutely no interest in you when you wear black pants, where your nose hears and your ears smell, and coffee puts you right to sleep.

CLOPRICRUMB

If all the staircases in the world were made of live alligators, then ascending and descending would be risky business. Folks would install fire poles and rope ladders in their houses to avoid losing a limb on a quick trip to the basement for fish sticks.

But you, my dear Goat Fish, you are a soft and empathetic creature. You would approach each alligator step, crouch down, pet it softly, let it know that you mean it no harm, looking deep into that alligator eye until you understand each other, and then proceed. It wouldn't be fast, but you could do it. Maybe you'd get a scratch or lose a toe now and then, but because you'd take your time with each reptilian beast, your alligator stairs would leave you be.

AQUARKIFLUS

What if all your friends turned into corn snakes, but it was OK because you learned to speak in their distinct hisses, and you kept super tasty frozen mice for them in your freezer, and the way they got sleepy after eating was just like before they were snakes, so it was all cool, you'd just adapt?

And really, if you could love your friends that much even if they were the wimps of the snake world, you must be doing pretty good at friendshipping, maybe better than you realize.

So reach out to your friends a bit extra this month, even if it's just a bonus meme or a superfluous hello. Get at them while they still have fingers and legs and endothermic blood—which, even if they don't turn into snakes, won't be forever.

PISCERRS

What is your morning routine? Some hygiene, a bit of sustenance, then off to the sewage treatment plant or to your workshop to whittle tiny wooden leprechauns or whatever it is you do?

Nonsense.

The twinklers and dazzlers out in space have wriggled into a flamboyant configuration just now, beckoning for you to shake up your morning routine and flop it around a little. Maybe try twinkling and dazzling your own sweet self.

Could you perhaps sleep in full parade regalia, spring out of bed, and lead a marching band for a block or two, and only *then* make your morning tea and crumpets? Could you set some fireworks off out your bathroom window to alert the world to your wakefulness prior to brushing your teeth with your usual hygienic diligence? At the very, and absolute *very* least, flick on some Pointer Sisters when first you wake so you can both jig and jiggle your way through your morning hours.

DECEMBER

December

*I*t's December, and the worst thing you can do now is take your foot off the gas and try to coast along, hoping inertia will carry you through the rest of the year. No, December is like a silent meditation retreat, only your whole family and everyone from middle school is there, and not only are *they* allowed to talk but they've all got megaphones pointed directly at you.

December isn't easy. The winter stomps in, dragging gloomy weather with it, and for some reason everyone thinks it's peachy to stuff your calendar with a million social obligations.

And as if there weren't enough hurdles, society has decided that you need thoughtful gifts for various friends, neighbors, coworkers, mothers, dogs, and mail carriers in order to keep judgmental glares and your own inward sense of guilt at bay. Oh capitalism, you naughty beagle!

December's saving grace is the solstice. Just when the days have dwindled to eighteen and a half seconds of daylight, the winter solstice comes along, wags her long finger at the sun, and says, "Hey now, you've tortured these pour Northern Hemispheric souls long enough. Let's give the Southern Hemisphere a taste of this rancid aspic-flavored misery, shall we?"

And the sun obeys, and the days start creeping ever longer. Because winter is hard, and darkness doubly so. The promise of longer days makes this challenging existence just a little easier.

December 22: Splattitaribus Season Out, Clopricrumb Season In

We spend most of the month dipped in the bubbling oils of a Splattitaribus fondue and feel it cooking our centaur meats. We all have a few centaur meats somewhere inside us, and if we let it, this season warms them in its bubbling oils and helps us stand tall like a mythic beast.

But soon this Splatty time will end like a cow inspecting the sea: firm and true and moist around the ankles.

And in comes that Clopricrumb energy! With the sturdiness of a mountain goat and the wiggle-wags of a mountain fish, we welcome our Goat Fish friends to the forefront of our feels.

This time is a cornucopia of ripening fruits. A Goat Fish is a balanced creature, like a yellow banana with the perfect glow of green still smiling from her peel, or a peach that gives in softly to the sharpness of your teeth as you plunge in with a bite, but not so much that it mushes in your mouth.

When you're clopping firmly this month, don't forget your wiggly fish energy. And when you're crumbling about, don't forget your sturdy goat. You're Cloppy. You're Crumbly. You're the embodiment of a Clopricrumb.

Holidays in December

December 11 *Make Soup for a Spider Day:* Remember, spiders eat bugs. You must make a tiny bowl of bug soup, with bug broth and a side of bug.

December 24 *Release as Much Familial Guilt as Humanly Possible Day:* Wow! This time of year can be weird. It can mess with our brains. Today we're letting some of that go, even if it's oddly tempting to hold on to grievances. Throw away those bad feelings like moldy leftovers.

December 26 *Order a Large Poster of Yourself Looking Happy While Playing a Sport Day:* Chances are, even with the various holidays and their gift-giving natures, you didn't receive anything good. So take a selfie, paste it on a photo of someone playing tennis or SlamBall (a real sport from the early 2000s), and give yourself the gift of a really good-looking poster. Cardboard cutouts are also acceptable and can be purchased from your local print shop. You deserve it.

December 30 *Overconfidence Day:* Compensate for all the days this year where you have had faltering and floundering confidence by swinging wildly in the other direction. Today is for uncharacteristic boldness, unearned faith in your own abilities, and a stubborn self-belief that remains no matter how much you fail.

December Journal Prompts

1. If you were a potato preparation, what potato preparation would you be? Scalloped? Mashed? Sculpted into tiny people with little hats made from mushrooms? What does this say about how deeply maladjusted you are as a person?

2. If—in a heroic and daring coup—you usurped control of Hallmark and the dreary onslaught of holiday movies they produce, what maniacal rom-com would you have them create in lieu of their usual bland fare?

3. The year is coming to an end; it's a time for reflection. Make a list of all the best toots you had this year, all the farts you valiantly held in for the olfactory comfort of others, the notable noisy flatulence of others you bore witness to, and all the times the whole world around you seemed to break wind all at once.

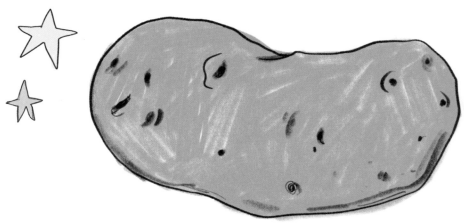

December Scoops

ARBYS

When winter digs her icy fingers in, many people reflexively run from her chilly grasp, taking refuge in warmer climates, maybe containing a plethora of palm trees and parrots and the sort of sun exposure that would make your dermatologist sweat even though she's three thousand miles away.

But whether you prance off to one such place, live there full time, or have never been so fortunate, remember that a chilly moment can liven up the Arbys Rammy spirit. Those long horns of yours can store creative energy, and nothing fills them up like a plunge into the thrilling abyss of freezing cold. Of course, this is all within reason. Safety first. But a little shiver up the spine tingles the creative brain cells and gets your most succulent mind juices squirting.

TORBUS

You are the twinkliest of snowflakes. The low winter sun glitters upon your mystifying myriad of frozen ice crystals as you drift down from the heavens. Not only are you wholly unique in your perplexing physical form, but the way you twirl and tumble from the sky with such odd near-gracefulness is purely you in that purely you way. You're doing a dance no dancer ever dared to dream before, a whirligig of fumbling and rumbling, a ruptured prance almost as if you were tripping and just barely catching yourself over and over as you spin yourself silly, my dear darling Bullish Babe.

And this unique snowflake dance you do—whatever it looks like to others—feels so dang good inside. You know when you're dancing your true snowflake whirligig dance because every ice crystal, every shining molecule in your being, glows with the glittering joyous light of being alive.

GERMINI THE TWRNNNS

Dawn approaches, though it is still dark, with a hint of indigo breaking through the black sky, striped with clouds. There is a cold, solid crust of ice here on the plains of the arctic tundra.

And yet somehow—impossibly—something new grows straight from the frozen ground, cracking through the crust of hard-packed ice and snow. As the darkness breaks, the sun creeps closer to the horizon, more of this desolate landscape becomes visible, and it's clear. There's something green here.

A flower grows in the dead of winter: a tulip, budding, nearly ready to bloom, with edges of color, pink and red, brighter than the scarlet sunrise that paints the flower as it slowly unfolds.

This tulip is you. Resilient against all odds, impossibly adaptable, capable of feats that no one ever thought possible. Inspiring in ways you may not realize. And, if I may—beautiful.

CONSUR

The year ends with you as a precious burrito.

Like a burrito, you are complex, full of rice and spice and things that are nice. Stuffed with an assortment of disparate flavors that come together to create one homogenous being more delicious and harmonious than any of your individual parts.

Like a burrito, you're wrapped tight and could crack and spill open at any moment. But also like a burrito, you would still be enjoyed and loved in your cracked and open state—you may even be more thrilling with a little spilly danger.

Like a burrito, you are snug.

Like a burrito, you find comfort in coziness, swaddled like an innocent infant or like an equally innocent burrito.

LEMO

You could make yourself a full-body poncho out of solid silver and gold pinecones, and it would be magnificent, but it would be quite heavy and cumbersome, and you'd barely be able to stand in it. All the effort that went into fashioning this solid-precious-metal poncho would be nothing compared to the efforts you'd need to go to strengthen your body to bear its weight. You'd need to spend months at the gym, squatting and pressing and this-ing and that-ing until you were strong enough to even slide it onto your body.

But there you'd be in your silver and gold pinecone poncho, standing regally, being stared at curiously by squirrels who would wonder if there's still a delicious pine nut in the middle of a golden pinecone. And you'd know whether the effort had all been worth it.

VURBO

The constellation of Oblurkus—the great space dumpling dog just east of Orion's naughty bits—opens up and unravels her unwieldy tongue. Down and down rolls the tongue, until, at last, it reaches the Earth. The cosmic space tongue extends from Oblurkus for a few brief weeks every December, to waggle upon the good Vurbos of the Earth and bless them with generous hearts and abundant spirits.

Not that you need a luscious lick from a cosmic space tongue to feel the spirit of generosity bubbling beneath your epidermis. You're a kind soul the whole year round. But oh! it is a delight, a damp and darling delight, to feel that spiritually moist nudge in an altruistic direction. You find yourself emotionally sticky from the interdimensional saliva that remains upon your being, and enlivened by its noble salivary gifts.

LEHBRAH

Secret messages are being transmitted to you in blinking holiday lights, messages that only Lehbrahs can decipher. They are subtle and subliminal and require a psychic and holistic approach to comprehend.

All I know for certain is that they're sent from the Sugar-Free Plum Fairies (who, contrary to the sound of their name, have such sweet demeanors that they don't need artificial saccharine enhancement).

The Fairies use the intermittent blinking of the world's holiday lights to send out a message, not so much in words as in feelings, in vibes, in a guttural instinctual knowledge. When you see twinkling holiday lights, feel them out. Receive their communication into your loins. You will understand, and you will know your mission.

SLURPEEO

This can be an overwhelming month, what with social obligations, traveling home, friends coming to visit, and family coming out your ears covered in earwax and then complaining about how waxy your ears are.

What you need is a quiet place in every situation. What you need is a cupboard.

Wherever you go, be it a family gathering or drinks at a bar, find yourself a cupboard. Maybe it's a cupboard under the bathroom sink, and you can nestle in the fetal position beside the Toilet Duck. Or maybe you climb on the counter in the middle of Uncle Jeremy's latest story about his many pet fruit bats and hoist yourself up into the kitchen cupboard that used to house your mother's good dinnerware before she took it all out to set the table.

If people have a problem with you being in a cupboard, know that deep down their real beef is that they didn't think of it first. Besides, they can't complain to you. You're in a cupboard.

SPLATTITARIBUS

Five times this month, a large, handsome stag will walk confidently ahead of you on your path in life, turn directly away, poop out a grapefruit (or another large citrus, possibly a pomelo), and then strut away as handsomely as he strutted in.

It is up to you to find these grapefruits (or pomelos, yuzus, etc.) if you wish to eat them. (I would recommend washing them thoroughly first. He is a magical stag, but pooped fruit is pooped fruit.)

CLOPRICRUMB

Once again, there are no gifts for you from Santa's workshop. The only prezzies coming from far up north are from Carbuncle, the holiday rat. "Who?" you ask. Well, I'll tell you.

Carbuncle, the holiday rat,
She's a little bit short, and a little bit fat.
She has a red bow tie and a candy cane cane.
She collects everything Santa flushes down the drain.

She lives in the sewers beneath the North Pole,
And Santa's workshop is not flushing coal.
The elves flush any toys with a flaw or a crack,
And Carbunkle snags them to fill her own sack.

She flies through the sewers on her golden toad,
Leaves every Clop a gift next to their commode,
Then flies back home in time for a nap,
Saying, "Happy holidays to all, now enjoy your crap."

AQUARKIFLUS

This month, you're going to feel an overwhelming urge to talk to or interact with any animal-shaped holiday decorations on people's lawns.

When you see an inanimate creature on a lawn—let's say a plastic deer—part of you will want to get out a carrot, belly crawl across this stranger's yard, try to feed the deer, whisper that it's a good lad, and give it a scratch on the withers.

You'll have an irrational desire not just to talk to these decorative critters but to tell them everything on your mind: to reveal your secret recipe for kimchi, to explain why you let a toot slip out in a car full of popular kids that time in high school, even though you were five minutes away from home and you were physically capable of holding it, and to ask if it knows what you should do with the rest of your life.

On some level, you know that they're just cheap, inanimate trash. On some level, you know they don't understand. But on another level, you are entirely certain they do.

PISCERRS

You float high above a frozen lake, looking down on all the happy people laughing and skating below. You feel safer floating up above.

A polar bear floats up beside you and asks, "Am I the problem? Am I why you're up here? Are you afraid a big ole bear might eat you if you're down there? Because I don't plan on eating you today."

"No," you reply, "it's not you."

"Then what? Why do you feel so safe and calm up here, floating above all those people? Shouldn't you be down there, laughing and playing with them?"

"Sometimes it's just nice to have a little distance from it all. To be honest, sometimes people are scary, scarier to my nervous system than the thought of a bear."

"That's wild. And what about them?"

"Chances are they're more concerned with something social or seemingly trivial than they are with you."

"Should I bust into their skating rink and remind them how scary a polar bear can be?" asks the bear.

"No," you reply, "just float up here with me for a while."

Acknowledgments

Wildly grateful to Callie Deitrick for taking a chance and messaging me out of the blue. You're brilliant, and I'm so lucky to have you and Wendy Sherman representing me in this wild world of books.

Huge thanks to Dena Rayess and Lizzie Vaughan at Chronicle Books for taking my scrappy, raw, word material and turning it into a real, live book that some poor person is now reading me gush about. But for real, look at how cool it is!

Whenever I left confusing clumps of contradictory words in a pile on the floor, Judith Riotto came through and patiently picked them up. Thank you for your care in editing this book.

My incredible partner, Nate Waters, has kept me well fed and full of encouragement and always reminds me that making art is supposed to be fun. My never-ending gratitude goes to him and to my fuzzier soulmate, Poppy.

Lana McCarroll, you've been there for me through so much for so long. I hit the friendship jackpot. You're the best. Thank you.

Grant and Michele, and Guy and Augusta, thanks for always filling me up with love and support.

To my mom, Christine, thanks for instilling in me a love of words, and sorry I spelled so many of them wrong in this book. To my dad, Guy, thanks for making sure I had a proper education in slapstick comedy. All that absurdity has served me well.

Dr. Belyea and Dr. Kang—not everyone is lucky enough to have their bizarre symptoms believed and taken seriously immediately, and I would not have been well enough (or in little enough pain) to write this without you both. Thank you.

To the folks at nvrlnd. Arts Foundation, you're more than just an art studio; you're my wonderfully weird art family. Thanks to you and all my other pals in the Calgary arts community.

And finally, an inconceivably large thank-you to everyone who has ever shared Horror Scoops online, whether it's every week or even just once. It's because of you that I had the opportunity to write all this nonsense. I am so deeply thankful to each and every one of you.